BedTime Stories

This Book Includes : "Bedtime Stories for Kids + Bedtime short Stories "

By Anna Smith

within is the solitary and utter responsibility of the recipient reader. Under no circumstances will any legal responsibility or blame be held against the publisher for any reparation, damages, or monetary loss due to the information herein, either directly or indirectly.

Respective authors own all copyrights not held by the publisher.

The information herein is offered for informational purposes solely and is universal as so. The presentation of the information is without contract or any type of guarantee assurance.

The trademarks that are used are without any consent and the publication of the trademark is without permission or backing by the trademark owner. All trademarks and brands within this book are for clarifying purposes only and are the owned by the owners themselves s, not affiliated with this document.

Bedtime Stories for Kids

Table of content

Bedtime Short Stories

Table of content

Bedtime Stories for Kids

A Collection of Bedtime Short Stories for Kids to Help You Fall Asleep Quickly.

By Anna Smith

Chapter 1: Bedtime Stories with Morals

Short stories teach children moral lessons. These get embedded in their young minds and they ponder upon them as they grow older. Besides, short stories are conducive for children's imaginative thinking and creativity. Short stories also help increase their vocabulary and develop their oral and written communication skills.

1.1 The Frogs & the Ox

An Ox has come down to drink from a reedy pool. He smashed a young Frog into the dirt, as he poured heavily into the water.

Soon the old Frog missed the little one and told his brothers and sisters what he had become.

"A great big man," said one of them, "walked up with one of his huge feet on the little boy!" "Huge, he was!" said the old Frog, puffing up. "Is he bigger than this?" exclaimed they, "Yeah, much bigger! "The Frog puffed up even more.

"He couldn't be taller than this," she said. Yet the little Frogs all proclaimed the beast to be much, much bigger and the old Frog kept puffing out more and more before she burst out, all at once.

Moral: You must not try for the impossible.

1.2 The Two Goats

Two goats chanced to meet on the rugged steeps of a mountain valley, one on either side of a deep gorge from which a mighty torrent of mountains poured. The only way to cross the chasm was the trunk of a fallen tree. It was so narrow that even two squirrels could not have passed each other in safety. The narrow road made the bravest tremble. Not so for our goats. Their pride will not allow one to stand aside for another either.

One laid her foot on the wood. The other did the same. They met horn to horn in the center. Neither would give way only to be swept away by the raging river below as they both fell.

Moral: Yielding is better than ending up in failure by stubbornness.

1.3 The Heron

A Heron walked calmly along a stream bank, his eyes on the clear water, and his long neck and pointed bill ready to catch a morsel for his breakfast. The clear water was swarming with fish but that morning Master Heron was hard to please

"No little fries for me," he said. "This scanty fare isn't fit for a Heron." A good young Perch swam nearby now.

"Not really," the Heron said. The Heron even detested opening its beak for petty fish. However, as

the sun rose, the fish left the shallow water near the shore. The fish swam down into the cool middle depths. The Heron no longer saw shrimp, so he had to be contented with a tiny snail.

Moral: Don't be too fussy or you would have to be happy with the worst, or with none.

1.4 The Eagle & the Beetle

Once upon a time a Beetle begged the Eagle to spare a Hare. The Hare had run to Beetle for safety. But the Eagle pounced on her prey, tumbling the Beetle a dozen feet away with the sweep of its great wings. Furious at her disrespect, the Beetle flew into the Eagle's nest and rolled the eggs out. She did not spare a single one. The sorrow and rage of the Eagle knew no bounds but she did not know who had done the cruel deed.

The Eagle built her nest on a mountain crag far up the next year; but the Beetle found it and killed the eggs once again. The Eagle now in desperation implored great Jupiter to let her put her eggs in his lap. None would venture to hurt them there. But the Beetle buzzed over Jupiter's head, and pulled him up to drive her away, and the eggs rolled off his lap.

Now the Beetle explained the reason for her action and Jupiter had to accept her cause's justice. And they conclude that ever since the Beetle still sleeps in the field while the Eagles eggs lie in the nest in spring. So, Jupiter ordered.

Moral: Even the weakest would find means to avenge a cruel act.

1.5 The Man & the Satyr

A Man encountered a Satyr in the forest a long time ago, and managed to make friends with him. The two soon became the best of friends, staying in the Man's hut together. Yet one cold winter evening the Satyr saw the Man blow on his fingers as they walked together.

"Why are you doing that?" the Satyr asked. "To keep my hands warm," replied the Man.

The Man made two bowls of porridge when they arrived home. He placed these on the table while these were steaming hot, and the comrades sat very cheerfully to enjoy the meal. But the Man started blowing into his bowl of porridge, much to the dismay of the Satyr

"Why are you doing this?" he asked.

"To cool my porridge," replied the Man.

Hurriedly the Satyr leaped to his feet and headed for the gates.

"Goodbye," he said, "I have seen enough. A fellow who blows hot and cold in the same breath can't be buddies with me!"

Moral: You cannot trust the man who speaks for both sides.

1.6 Hercules & the Wagoner

There was a Farmer. Once, he was driving his wagon along a miry country road after a hefty rain. The equines can hardly drag the lots via the deep mud, and also at last stopped when one of the wheels got stuck into the rut's hub.

The Farmer had to climb down from his seat. He also stood close to the wagon cursing him and without making the least initiative to do anything about it. He only cursed his bad luck as well as called noisily on Hercules for his aid. It is stated, Hercules really did appear, claiming:

"Put your shoulder to the wheel, guy, and make your horses move. You are wrong if you think you can move the wagon by merely watching and also grumbling regarding it? Hercules will not aid unless you take some initiative to help on your own."

So, when the Farmer placed his shoulder to the wheel and urged on the horses, the wagon moved really conveniently and quickly. The Farmer finally rode along in great content. The Farmer also learned an excellent lesson.

Self-help is the very best help.

Moral: Heaven assists those who assist themselves.

1.7 The Bundle of Sticks

There was a father who had a family comprising of Sons. His sons were permanently quarreling among themselves. No words he can claim did the least significant, so he thought in his mind for some incredibly striking example that ought to make them see that discord would lead them to misfortune.

Eventually when the quarreling had been a lot more terrible than typical as well as each of the Sons was behaving in a surly fashion, he asked one of them to bring him a bundle of sticks. Handing the package to each of his Boys in turn he informed them to attempt to break it. However, although everyone tried his finest, none was able to do so.

The Father then un-knotted the package and gave the sticks to his Sons to break them one by one. This they did very easily.

" My Boys," stated the Dad, "do you not see just how specific it is that if you agree with each other as well as aid each other, it will be difficult for your enemies to injure you? However, if you are split among yourselves, you will certainly be no stronger than a single stick in that bundle."

Moral: Unity is strength

1.8 The Ass & the Load of Salt

A Merchant was driving his Ass homeward from the seaside with a hefty load of salt. He came to a river crossed by a shallow ford. They had actually crossed this river lot of times before without accident, however this time around the Ass slid as well as dropped after he had crossed halfway. And when the Merchant finally brought him to his feet, much of the salt had actually dissolved. Delighted to discover just how much lighter his problem had become; the Ass finished the trip really happily.

Following day, the Merchant went for another tons of salt. While he was coming back home, the Ass recalled what had actually happened at the ford, and intentionally allowed himself to fall into the water, and thus got rid of most of his load.

The angry Merchant quickly turned about and drove the Ass back to the seaside, where he filled him with two large baskets of sponges. At the ford the Ass once more toppled over; but when he had scrambled to his feet, it was a despondent Ass that dragged himself homeward under a load that was ten times larger than the previous load.

Moral: The very same actions will not match all scenarios.

1.9 The Leap at Rhodes

A particular man that visited foreign lands might talk of little when he went back to his home other than the remarkable experiences he had actually met with as well as the great actions he had actually done abroad.

Among the accomplishments he talked about was a jump he had actually made in a city Called Rhodes. That leap was so excellent, he claimed, that no other man could leap anywhere near the distance. A great many persons in Rhodes had actually seen him do it as well as would certainly prove that what he informed was true.

"No requirement of witnesses," said one of the hearers. "Expect this city is Rhodes. Currently reveal us exactly how far you can leap."

Moral: Acts count, not boasting words.

1.10 The Mice & the Weasels

In every fight the Weasels carried off the success, as well as a huge number of the mice, which they ate for supper the following day. In misery the Mice called a council, and there it was determined that the army of the mice was always beaten because it had no leaders.

To identify themselves from the soldiers in the ranks, the new leaders happily bound on their heads soaring crests and accessories of plumes or straw. After that lengthy preparation of the Mouse army in all the arts of battle, they sent a challenge to the Weasels.

The Weasels accepted the task with eagerness, for they were always all set for a fight when a meal was in sight. They immediately attacked the Mouse army in high numbers. Quickly the mouse line gave way prior to the assault as well as the whole military fled for cover. The Weasels quickly got on their openings, yet the Mouse leaders cannot pass through the narrow openings because of their head-dresses. Not one mouse could run away from the teeth of the hungry Weasels.

Moral: Greatness has its penalties

1.11 The Dog & His Master's Dinner

A Pet Dog had actually discovered to lug his master's supper to him each day. He was extremely loyal to his duty, though the smell of the good things in the basket attracted him.

The dogs in his area discovered him bring the basket and also quickly found what the Dog used to carry in it. They made numerous attempts to take it from him. But he always guarded it consistently.

Then eventually, all the dogs in his area got together and also met him on his way with the basket. The Dog attempted to run away from them. He finally dropped the basket and stood to argue with the dogs.

That was his blunder. They quickly made him feel so ludicrous that he dropped the basket as well as got hold of roast meat intended for his master's dinner.

"Very well," he claimed, "you split the remaining food."

Moral: Do not argue with temptation.

1.12 The Two Pots

There were two Pots, one of brass and the other one of clay. They stood together on the hearthstone. One day the Brass Pot asked to the Earthen Pot that they go out right into the world together. The Earthen Pot excused himself, saying that it would certainly be smarter for him to stay in the corner by the fire.

"It would take so little to damage me," he claimed. "You know exactly how vulnerable I am. The least shock makes sure to smash me!"

"Don't let that keep you in the house," urged the Brass Pot. "I shall take great care of you. If we ought to go to a place to meet anything tough, I will step between and conserve you."

The Earthen Pot finally gave in to Brass demand, and the two set out side by side, jolting along on three short legs initially to one side, then to the other side. They bumped into each other at every step.

The Earthen Pot was unable to survive that sort of companionship very long. They had actually not gone ten paces before the Earthen Pot broke, and at the following jolt, he broke right into a thousand pieces.

Moral: Equals make the best close friends.

1.13 The Spendthrift & the Swallow

A young man, who as a good spender and was highly popular among his boon friends, lost his fortune quickly trying to live up to his reputation. Then he found himself one fine day early in the spring with no penny left, and no property but the clothes he wore.

That morning, he was going to meet some beautiful young men and he was at the end of his wits, how to get enough money to keep up appearances. Just then a Swallow flew by, merrily twittering, and the young man, feeling that summer had arrived, rushed to a clothes dealer, to whom he sold all the clothes he was wearing down to his very tunic.

A few days later a change of weather brought heavy frost. As a result, the swallow and the unwise young man in his light tunic, and with his arms and knees bare, could hardly hold life in their shivering bodies.

Moral: The summer is not ushered in by one Swallow

1.14 The Milkmaid & Her Pail

A Milkmaid used to milk the cows. One day when she had a lot of milk, she was returning from the field, standing beautifully on her head with the shiny milk pail. As she walked along her beautiful head was busy with plans for the days ahead.

"This sweet, rich milk," she mused, "will give me plenty of churning cream. I'll take the butter I make to the market, and with the money I get for it I'll buy a lot of eggs. How pleasant it will be when they're all hatched, and the yard is full of fine young chicks. Then when the good days come, I'll sell them, and with the money I'll buy a pretty new dress to wear at the fair. I will be the center of attention for all men and they would try to get my love—but I shall very quickly send them about their business!" While she was thinking, she was also tossing her head as a result of which all the milk poured out. Thus, the butter and chicks and eggs and a new dress and the joy of the milkmaid vanished with it.

Moral: Do not count the chickens until they are hatched

1.15 The Miser

A Miser had buried his gold in his backyard, in a hidden location. He went to the spot every day, uncovered the treasure and counted it piece by piece to make sure it was all there. He made so many trips that a Robber, who had been watching him, realized what the Miser had concealed, and secretly dug up the treasure one night and ran away.

He was overwhelmed with sorrow and despair, when the Miser realized his loss. He groaned and wept.

A passerby listened to his cry and asked what had happened.

"My gold! Oh, my gold!" the Miser screamed desperately, "someone has robbed me!" "Your gold! In that hole?" Why did you put it there? Why didn't you keep it in the house where you could easily get it when you needed to buy things?" "Buy and what!" the Miser screamed angrily. "Why, I never touched the gold." The stranger picked up a big stone and hurled it into the cave.

"If that's the case," he said, "cover the stone. It's worth just as much for you as the gold you've lost!"

Moral: Any possession is worth only its utility.

1.16 The Rose & the Butterfly

A Butterfly dropped in love with a gorgeous Rose. The Rose was not indifferent, for the Butterfly's wings were powdered in a lovely pattern of gold and silver.

But alas! It was a long time before he returned to her.

"It is ages since you went away, as well as all the time, you have actually been carrying on with all kinds of blossoms. I saw you kiss Miss Geranium, and also you fluttered around Miss Mignonette till Honey Bee chased you away.

You carried on scandalously with Mr. Bumble Bee and you made eyes at every solitary insect you can see. You cannot expect any type of consistency from me!"

Moral: Do not anticipate consistency in others if you have none on your own.

1.17 The Porcupine & the Snakes

A Porcupine was searching for a great house. Finally, he found a little protected cave, where lived a family member of Snakes. He asked to allow him to share the cave with them, and the Snakes kindly consented.

The Snakes quickly desired they had actually not offered him permission to remain in their home with them. His sharp quills hurt and wounded them at every turn as well. After going through this trouble, they finally decided to ask the snake to leave politely. The snake said that he was quite comfortable in that place and asked them to leave the place instead.

As well as with that, he nicely escorted the Snakes out of doors. To save their skins, the Snakes had to look for another residence.

Moral: Offer a finger and sacrifice a hand.

1.18 Jupiter & the Monkey

Once there was a baby show program among the animals of the forest to select the cutest of the babies. Jupiter supplied the prize. Certainly, all the happy Mammas from far and near brought their infants. However, none arrived earlier than Mommy Ape. Happily, she presented her baby to the other participants.

As you can think of, there was quite a laugh when the Animals saw the hideous flat-nosed, hairless, pop-eyed little animal.

"Laugh if you will," claimed the Mom Ape. "Though Jupiter might not give him the prize, I recognize that he is the prettiest, the sweetest, my dearest beloved in the world."

Moral: Mother love is blind.

1.19 The Lion's Share

A long period of time back, the Lion, the Fox, the Jackal, and also the Wolf consented to go hunting with each other. They also decided to share with each other whatever they located and hunted.

Eventually the Wolf got hold of a Stag and as well as instantly called his pals to separate the spoil equally.

Without being asked, the Lion put himself ahead of the feast to do the carving, and, with a terrific show of fairness, started to count the visitors.

"One," he claimed, counting on his claws, "that is me the Lion. Two, that's the Wolf, three, is the Jackal, and also the Fox makes the four."

He then very carefully and thoroughly divided the Stag into four equal components.

"I am King Lion," he claimed, when he had completed, "so naturally I obtain the first component. This following part falls to me due to the fact that I am the best; and also, this is mine since I am the bravest."

He now started to glare at the others really savagely. "If any of you have any claim to the component that is left," he growled, extending his claws in a mean way, "currently is the time to speak out."

Moral: Might is right

Chapter 2: Fairy Tales

Fairy tales teach children life lessons. Fairy tales improve a child's imagination and cultural literacy, which is much powerful and essential. Fairy tales often depict different cultures and ways of doing good things. They teach the difference between right and wrong by strong moral lessons. Fairy tales help to create an ability in children, which paves the way for an understanding of what is right and what is wrong, not through direct teaching, but implication. Fairy tales teach children that good will always triumph.

Fairy tales develop critical thinking skills in kids. They learn about what happens to them, depending on the choices they make. These stories teach them to make good decisions, even at bad times for a better ending. Fairy tales can help children deal with their anxiety. Children relate these stories and find a fairy tale hero in themselves. Also, fairy tales are great fun taking the kids to another world of dragons, prince, kingdom, palace, castle, etc. These are memories of overwhelming excitement for your children if they really enjoy and grasp the real content of fairy tales.

2.1 The Fish and the Ring

There once was a powerful Baron who had a magic book. With it, he could see the future. He was unhappy to see in his book a baby girl from a poor family who would be his son's wife. He went to the father of the girl and offered to help take care of the baby girl. The father gave the baby to him, and the Baron took her away on his horse.

On his way home, the Baron threw the baby girl into the river, but she didn't die. She floated down the river and was rescued by a fisherman. The fisherman took her home and raised her. One day, the Baron and some friends went to the fisherman's hut to have a drink. A young girl brought drinks to the men, and they talked about how beautiful she was. One of them asked the Baron to tell who she would marry. When the Baron asked where the girl had been born, she said she only knew that she was saved from the river fifteen years before. The Baron knew right away that it was the girl he had tried to kill.

The Baron later returned to the fisherman's hut and asked the girl to deliver a letter to his brother. He said he would pay her well. The girl did not know that the letter was an order to the Baron's brother to kill her. On the way to deliver the letter, she stayed in a country inn. Some robbers broke into the inn, but they found no money on the girl. She only had the letter. They felt sorry for her after they read the letter, and the head robber decided to help her. He rewrote the letter, telling the Baron's brother to have the Baron's son marry the girl. The son and the girl were married as soon as the brother saw the letter.

After the wedding, the Baron visited his brother. When he came to know that it was his son had married the poor girl, he was shocked. He asked the girl to go for a walk with him on the cliffs. He tried to throw her into the sea, but she begged for her life. The Baron let her go, but before he did, he threw his gold ring into the sea and told the girl never to return without that ring.

The girl walked a long way before coming to a nobleman's castle. She begged for work and was made a cook. One day, she was surprised to see the Baron and her husband at the castle. She had to cook a meal for them. While preparing a fish, she saw a gold ring in the fish's mouth. It was the ring the Baron had thrown into the sea. The girl was excited. The meal was delicious, and the guests wanted to know who the cook was.

When the girl came out, the Baron was surprised and angry. He wanted to hit her, but she smiled and calmly showed him the ring on her finger. Then she took it off and put it on the table. At last, the Baron understood that he could not change the future. He then smiled and proudly introduced his daughter-in-law to the other guests. The Baron went home with his son and daughter-in-law, and everyone lived happily ever after.

2.2 A Christmas Carol

Young Scrooge had once kept busy in his office on Christmas Day. It was really cold outdoors, and not much better at Scrooge's workplace either.

Then a nephew of Scrooge walked into the room. "Have a happy Holiday, Dad! Save thy God! "And Fred said."Baaaa! "Scrooge said:" Humbug! ". "Humbug on Christmas, dad! "Scrooge's nephew said. "I am sure you don't mean that? "And I do," Scrooge said. "What is the season of Christmas to you? No income, you have to pay bills! You are a year older but not wealthier than before! Hold in your way Christmas, and let me have it in mine." "Hold it? But you don't have it, "said the nephew of Scrooge, who had become a really nice young man. He also attempted to cheer Scrooge up on Christmas Day and hosted him for dinner. Yet Scrooge said no to him and showed him outside.

As the nephew left Scrooge, two gentlemen walked in to raise funds for the needy who had no place to go. Stingy Scrooge however offered little money to the gentlemen. "There are no jails up there? There are no workhouses up there? "He begged them to leave the office sarcastically.

Scrooge was chatting to his assistant, Bob Cratchit, when it came time to leave the door. "You want the entire day off tomorrow, don't you? "Scrooge said. "If that is all correct, Sir," the clerk responded. "It's not all right," Scrooge said, "and it's just not fair. After all, while you aren't employed, I have to compensate you for the day. But if it has to be, I want you to get to work much early the next morning. "Cratchit said he would go home and the two went home.

Scrooge once lived in an old building all alone. That night, the yard was really dark and creepy, and when Scrooge tried to open the door, he had the sensation of seeing there the spirit of his old business associate Marley, who died a long time ago. It was really spooky so it wasn't easy for Scrooge to be afraid. "Humbug," he said, raising the door and stepped in. Nevertheless, he shut himself in, something he normally could not do.

But then again, he felt safe, and sat before the flames. Suddenly, as if someone was pulling a heavy chain, Scrooge heard a noise, down below.

The movement got louder and near and then Scrooge noticed a ghost come through the big door straight through. It was the ghost of Marley and his chains were thick, made of cash-boxes, keys and heavy purses. "Who are you, then? "Scrooge said. "I was your partner in creation, Jacob Marley." "So now why do you come to me? "Because I was too stingy in practice, I have to walk around the universe and carry chains. I was always thinking about business but not the people around me. I'm here, now, to alert you. You do have time, Ebenezer. There will come to you three Spirits. Expect the first day, when the bell tolls one. "Marley's spirit vanished after he had spoken these words; and the night became silent again. Scrooge went directly to bed, without undressing and promptly fell asleep.

It was already very foggy and very cold when Scrooge awakened, so there was no sign of people throughout the road. The spirit of Marley had disturbed him. Scrooge could not figure out whether it was a dream or a real-life event. And he recalled at one o'clock a ghost would be meeting him. And Scrooge wanted to lay awake, hoping to see what will happen.

Suddenly one clock reached. Light lit up in the room and his bed curtains were pulled back by a little hand. Scrooge suddenly finds himself meeting the stranger face to face. It was a strange image – like a boy: but not so much like a kid as an old lady. Her hair was white as though of age, flowing about her neck and down her back; and yet her face had no wrinkle in it. "Who are you? "The ghost was questioned by Scrooge. "I am Christmas Present Angel. Get up and come with me.

"Scrooge was taken back in time by the ghost, to a place Scrooge was a boy. There Scrooge could see his younger self enjoying himself with other kids. They were playing around the Christmas tree in a joyful manner; and while mediocre, they had a lot of fun.

Scrooge was even carried by the spirit to a factory, where Scrooge was a student. Scrooge witnessed the happy Christmas Eve they and their manager Mr. Fezziwig and his relatives enjoyed in the shop. There was nourishment and music and dance and everybody was content.

Once again, the ghost brought Scrooge to a new location again. Already Scrooge was getting older. He was not alone but was sitting by a stunning young girl's side, Belle. Her eyes were filled in tears. "Watch," she said quietly, "It is painful. "I have been replaced by this other passion – the passion of gold. Your heart was once full with passion, but now...? I guess we ought to split stronger. May you be content with your chosen life?" "Soul, "Scrooge said," show me no more. I want to go home. For what are you torturing me? "Just one more shadow," the ghost said.

They were in a different scene and place; a bed, not very large or magnificent but full of warmth. Happy families were enjoying Christmas with all their love and spirit. Scrooge recalled his old partner Belle. Now she was married and had kids. "Spirit, "Scrooge said in a distorted voice," Take me home! Can no longer stand it. "He tried to move out of the place. And Scrooge finally found himself back in his own home. He became tired and fell into a deep sleep.

Scrooge ended up in the midst of a snore, right as the clock again hit. He stood up in his bed waiting for the second ghost to appear. And it was there-the Christmas Present ghost. It had flowing brown hair, sparkling eyes and wore a plain, white-fur green robe. His feet were flat, and he carried a holly wreath over his cheek.

The ghost carried Scrooge to the house of Bob Cratchit-a really sad little home. You could see Mrs. Cratchit in the kitchen cooking for Christmas dinner. Her children played about cheerfully and Bob Cratchit came in on his back with Tiny Tim. Tiny Tim was youngest son of Bob Cratchit. He carried a wooden crutch and had an iron ring across his lower legs.

Then Christmas dinner was ready, and all were sitting down at the table. There wasn't anything they had for Christmas dinner, since the Cratchits were very poor. Yet everybody was always happy and you could tell that they still had the love of Christmas in their souls. "For all of us a Happy Christmas, loved people! May God help us! "Bob Cratchit said. "God save us all! "Tiny Tim said. He stood on his little bench, very close to his father's side. Bob squeezed his little side, as if he was scared of missing him.

"Ghost," said Scrooge, who was sad for the child, "tell me if Tiny Tim is going to stay." "I see an empty bench," the spirit answered, "and a crutch without an owner. The kid will die if those shadows don't shift in the future.

This made Scrooge quite unhappy but the spirit moved ahead, bringing Scrooge to the house of his nephew. Fred and his mates were holding a very fun party and had played football. Scrooge still liked their group and wished to live for another time but it all vanished in a second and Scrooge and the spirit were on their journey again.

Scrooge immediately discovered something peculiar about the spirit. Two characters like children were at the foot of the phantom-a boy and a girl. Yet, they seemed like tiny dolls, ancient and horrible. Shocked was Scrooge. "Are they your people, spirit? "Asked Scrooge. "We are the creations of God," the spirit said "The child is Ignorance. Want is a kid. Beware of them all, but beware of this boy most of all, "the spirit said. "Did they have no place to go? "And Scrooge inquired. "There are no jails up America? There are no workhouses in there? "Spirit turned to Scrooge with phrases of its own.

The bell hit 12. The Christmas Present spirit has mysteriously disappeared. And Scrooge saw the third ghost coming towards him at the last stroke of the bell. The spirit comes nearer gradually and in silence. It was quite tall and wearing a deep black piece of clothing that concealed the whole body, allowing little to be seen except an extended side. "Are you Christmas Ghost? "Scrooge said, 'I'm more scared of you than any other demon.' The ghost didn't utter a thing, so Scrooge became frightened. They walked through the town and Scrooge heard several men talking about a dead person. Scrooge recognized that the people were worried and decided to find out. Yet the spirit kept moving.

The ghost took Scrooge down the streets familiar to him; and as they went together, Scrooge glanced around here and there to see himself, but he was not to be found anywhere. They went into the house of poor Bob Cratchit and saw by the fire the mother and the baby. Tranquil. Very relaxed. The tiny loud Cratchits were as silent as statues. The kids were hurrying to meet him when Bob Cratchit walked in. Then the two young Cratchits placed their little cheeks on his face as if to say, "Don't mind it, dad. Don't be sad. "Today you go in there? "His wife said.

"Indeed, my friend," Bob said again. "I wish you had left. Knowing how beautiful the environment is must have done you well. Yet you can see that often. I told him we'd be riding there every Sunday. My little, little boy. "Bob said. "My child." He broke down in tears.

He did not support her. Had he been willing to stop it, maybe he and his child may have been further separated than they were.

The spirit went away, bringing Scrooge into a churchyard. The ghost was standing between the graves and pointing down to one. Scrooge gradually moved for it and wrote his own name, Ebenezer Scrooge, on the stone of the cemetery, pursuing the ghost's tip.

"Holy Spirit! "Scrooge screamed," hear me. I am not the guy I used to be! I'm not going to be the guy I would have been up to now! If I am beyond all hope, why give me this? Nice Spirit, in my heart I'm going to celebrate Christmas and strive to hold that all year round. I'm living in the past, in the present and in the future. Within me would be the souls of these three. I am not going to dismiss the lessons they give. Yeah, just tell me I should alter my destiny! "Full of terror Scrooge grasped the side of the ghost. But the energy shifted abruptly-it decreased and diminished and eventually transformed into a bedpost.

Hey! And that had been his own bedpost. The bed was his own, its own space. The moment before him was his own life and happiness of all and he should make the best of it. "I'm going to live in the past, in the present and in the future," Scrooge said as he got out of bed.

"I have no idea what to do! I'm good, like an angel! I don't recognize the day of the month. I don't know how long I've been with these ghosts. Yo! Hallo! Hello there!

76

"He went up to the window, unlocked it, and put his head out. "What's this today? "Scrooge screamed, throwing a kid in Sunday clothes down. "Today? "And the boy responded. "This is the day of Christmas! "Scrooge said to himself. "I really didn't hear it! The spirits did all of this in one session. Hi, my favorite! Will you lean in the corner of the poulterer's? And do you know if the big turkey that hung up there was sold out? "What, the large one like me? "The man came back. "Now it's still lying out there." "Is it! "Scrooge said. "Go and get them! I'm sure. Go and purchase it, then come back to the man so I can show them the direction to take. For that, I will give you a shilling. Come back in under five minutes with the guy and I'll give you half-a-crown! "The kid took off like a rocket.

"I am going to give it to Bob Cratchit," Scrooge muttered cheerfully. "It's twice Tiny Tim's height." He dressed in all his charm, and finally got out onto the road.

When he got to the two gentlemen, who had come into his office the day before, he hadn't gone far. "My poor Boy," Scrooge replied, "How are you doing? I am sure yesterday I was not good to you. Let me ask you forgiveness. And you'll have the goodness to ... "Scrooge whispered in his ear here. "Bless me, O Lord! "The gentlemen called out," My poor Mr. Scrooge, are you serious? I don't know what to do about such kindness.

"He went to his nephew's house in the afternoon. "Fred," Scrooge said, "It's your uncle Scrooge. I have finished dinner. Do you want to call me stay, Fred? "Fred let him in, of course; it was a really warm welcome and they all had a great session.

But next thing, Scrooge was out at the workplace early. Yeah, he was in there early. If Bob Cratchit could just spot him arriving late. And it did; yeah, it did. Bob was a whopping eighteen and a half minutes behind his pace. Scrooge sat wide open with his windows, and he could see him entering.

"Good luck! "Scrooge grumbled, in his usual way. "What do you mean by coming at this hour of the day? I will no longer stand this sort of thing. And so, "he started, springing from his seat," and I'm about to increase your pay. A happy Christmas, Bob. "Bob Cratchit was really shocked that so many people thought that Scrooge had improved too much.

Scrooge was a decent human being. He was a second parent to Tiny Tim, who did not die.

Scrooge was a good dad, a good boss, and a decent guy, as the good old town understood, or every good old town in the good old country. And for Scrooge, it was always claimed that he knew how to enjoy Christmas. Can it be always said of us, and of us all! And so, as Tiny Tim will claim, may God bless us all!

2.3 The Three Princesses

There used to be three lovely princesses once. Their names were Kimmy, Kristen and Katie. Kimmy was three, Katie was five and Kristen was eight.

They were all staying in a manor, with butlers, maids, chefs and several men. Yet the princesses were not treating them as prisoners, they were handling them with love and compassion.

The mothers' name was Krystal. She was really caring, showing her three girls how to handle others with love and dignity. Mother had black hair that floated thick.

The father's name of the princess was Kevin. He taught his three girls how to be lady. He had blonde hair like guy. He was a really attractive guy.

They had a mentor called ken, as well. He had rich brown eyes. He was pretty beautiful.

A messenger came along one bright morning with really sad news. Mother's mother was very sick. Mum and dad needed to leave.

They left and the princesses lived with the uncle. For everyone the uncle was really rude. His attitude made all but the princesses uncomfortable at the manor.

He once ordered the chef that they should make steak and spaghetti. The uncle changed his mind, but told the cook not. The chef couldn't read minds and he was only cooking what the uncle wanted him to cook. The uncle got angry when he learned about the cook. The cook was not either happy with the uncle. Still Kristen assured him it was all right and the cook felt easier. Everybody ate lovingly what he had made and it tasted delicious.

One day the butler prepared the beds as normal, but he didn't like what he saw when the uncle examined them so he blew up at the butler making him look horrible. Kristen witnessed this event. He told the butler it was OK after the uncle departed. She made the butler feel better.

He did so to the maids, and perhaps to several people. One day after dinner Kristen talked about these scenes to her two little sisters. The girls decided to hold a conference in their tree house to decide ways to make uncle understand a lesson just like they had been instructed to be polite to compassionate to others.

Hoping to teach him a good lesson, the girls developed a proposal to be really nice to teach uncle a lesson.

Next day, they said to the chef, "Thank you for our food, this is a very good lunch," before enjoying their food. While the uncle sees his niece's friendly actions, he feels bad because he had never mentioned something pleasant or friendly to the chef.

The girls decided to help their very unique butler with his duties later that day. The Uncle sees this action and responds with rage ordering the girls to spend the rest of the day sitting in their beds. He doesn't want the girls to help butler with his work.

The furious uncle heads into the library and started thinking of how he acted towards the butlers, the maids, the cooks and even his three poor nieces, whom he made quite unhappy.

After the uncle had pondered well over his past rude behavior with everyone around, he let the girls have a conversation with them in the living room.

"The past few weeks, I have been behaving stupidly. I screamed at the chefs, the maids and the butlers. I wasn't respectful to anyone at the manor. Watching the three of you be respectful and pleasant to others, has inspired me to be compassionate and to respect others too. I am really grateful to you for showing me the right path, and I'm so sorry I haven't been too good to you. "Thanks to their dad, the girls are glad they made him realize him the value of reverence, grace, and affection.

A messenger came the next day and announced that the mother and father would be home in a few days and that their grandmother was much stronger.

For the remainder of his time with the girls the uncle was on his best behavior.

The mother and father have never learnt anything about the bad behavior of the uncle with their little princesses. The girls kept a silence on this. Just their children, and the children of their husbands, were told about the story. So, the experience has been passed on too many, many others.

2.4 The Princess and the Pea

There was once a boy who had been searching for a princess to wed. Yet he didn't want to marry any old girl, and he was searching for a princess. He traveled all over the world trying to seek the one. He knew several princesses but none of them fulfilled the criteria to be his future wife.

The prince had to return home without marrying a bride, which left him extremely sad.

There was a horrific storm outside one evening. There were thunderclaps and lightning lights. In the middle of the wind, someone pounded at the castle gates. A cute girl was standing there. Water was streaming out of her hair and clothes, but she confidently remained outside the door, saying she was a princess.

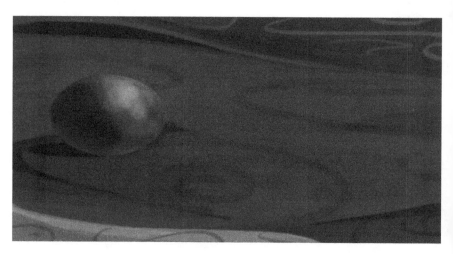

When the Queen discovered this, she immediately came up with a plan to test if the child really was a princess. She returned to the bedroom and put a pea in the middle of the bed. Then she piled on top of the pea twenty mattresses. This is where the child was staying for the night.

They told the princess the next morning if she had fallen asleep. "I couldn't sleep too well to be truthful. I looked as though I'd been sitting on a strong slope. My body is hurting from it too badly today, "she responded.

It was what the Queen was looking for. Everyone knew that the girl was a real princess because across twenty mattresses, she could sense the pea. It could have been sensed only by a real princess of extremely delicate skin.

Finally, the prince grinned and asked her to marry him, confident he had met the very princess he was searching for. The tied the nuptial knot and lived happily ever since.

2.5 Aladdin and the Wonderful Lamp

Aladdin lived in an eastern region. His father was a poor tailor. He was a lazy child, who liked to play rather than work; so that when his father Mustapha died, he did not make his living; who his poor mother had to spin cotton all day long to purchase food to sustain them. But she cherished her son deeply, believing he had a good heart, and she hoped he would do better when he grew older, and at last become a respectable and successful individual.

One day, as Aladdin was walking outside the house, an old man came up to him and looked really hard in his face, claiming he was the brother of his father and had been living in a far-off country for a long time, but now he wanted to help his nephew get on with his life. He then placed a ring on the boy's finger, promising him that as long as he kept it no harm will come to him. Oh, this mysterious man was not Aladdin's uncle, nor was he connected to him at all; but he was an evil wizard, as we shall see in a moment, who wished to make use of the lad's services.

The old man guided Aladdin through the country a good way, before they arrived at a very desolate place between two high black mountains. He lit a fire here, and put some gum into it, chanting several odd terms all the while. The earth then opened right before them, and there emerged a trap-door in stone. After raising this up, the Sorcerer instructed Aladdin to go down, down several broken stairs, and at the foot of these he would see three doors, in the last of which there was a door. The door was leading to a garden full of lovely trees; this he would pass, and after ascending a few more stairs he would come to a terrace where he would see a tiny shelf in which there was a lighted lamp. He was then to take the Candle, put the light out, drain the gasoline, and take it with him.

Aladdin noticed that everything the Magician had instructed him to be true; he went through the three halls rapidly but carefully so as not even to strike his clothes on the walls, as the Magician had guided. He picked up the Lamp from the table, poured the oil out and covered it in his jacket. When he walked back into the yard, the bright-colored fruits on the trees were dazzling his vision, sparkling like mirrors. He plucked many of these and placed them in his pockets, and then returned with the Torch, and called on his uncle to help him up the damaged stairs.

"Give me the Torch," the old man said, angrily.

"Not before I get out safely," the boy wept.

The Magician then slammed down the trap-door in rage and Aladdin was shut up fast enough. While weeping bitterly, he rubbed the ring by accident, and a figure appeared before him, saying, "The Genius of the Ring, I am at your command; what do you desire? "Aladdin told the Ring's Genius that he wished only to be set free and taken back to his mother. He felt himself very hungry at home in a moment and his poor mother was very happy to see him again. He told her everything that had happened, so she felt intrigued to look at the lamp that he had bought, and began rubbing it, to make it shinier. Both were very surprised to see a mysterious person emerging before them; this appeared to be the Lamp's Genius, who had called for their orders. Once they learned that food was what they needed most, a servant suddenly entered a dainty silver bowl with the most exquisite meals, so they had silver plates to feed from.

Aladdin and his mother offered them a feast on the rich fare and sold the silver dish and plates on the earnings they lived happily for a few weeks.

So, Aladdin was able to dress properly, so one day he chanced in on his regular stroll to see the Sultan's daughter emerging from the baths with her attendants. He was so impressed by her appearance that he instantly fell in love with her and told his mother she needed to go to the Sultan to persuade him to finalize his marriage with the Princess.

The poor mother said he must be crazy; but her son not only realized what a gem he had in the Magic Lamp, but he also noticed how precious the gleaming fruits he had picked were, which he believed were just colored glass at the time. At first, he submitted a bowlful of these jewels — for so they were — to the Sultan, who was delighted at their abundance, and said to Aladdin's mother: "Your son will have his wish, if he can give me forty bowls like this in a week, with twenty white and twenty black attendants, beautifully dressed." With this he wished to retain everything he had, and to no longer hear of Aladdin.

But the Lamp's Creator soon carried the jewel bowls and the staff, and Aladdin's mother went to the Sultan along with them.

The Sultan was overjoyed to obtain such rich presents, and decided at once that Aladdin's companion would be the Princess Bulbul. The delighted youth then called the Lamp's Genius to support him; and they soon set out for the Palace. He was dressed in a beautiful clothes suit, and mounted a magnificent horse; a number of officers marched by his side, spreading handfuls of gold among the men.

As soon as they were together, Aladdin instructed the Lamp's Genius to create a most magnificent Palace in the span of a week, and for some time the young couple lived there very happily.

One day, as Aladdin was out with the Pharaoh, the evil Magician, who had learnt of his good luck and tried to get hold of the Magic Lamp, screamed on the sidewalks, "Brand new lamps for old lamps!

"Hearing this, a dumb maid in the Palace got permission from the Princess to change Aladdin's old light, which she had seen on a stand where he often went, for a new one, and then the Magician took hold of it.

He forced the Genius to send the Castle, and Bulbul inside it, to Africa as soon as the Magician had safely received the Lamp.

Aladdin's sorrow was very strong, and so was the Sultan's frustration at the Princess's death, and the future of poor Aladdin was in considerable risk, for the Sultan tried to destroy him if he did not locate his daughter within three days.

Aladdin then turned to the Ring's Creativity to support him but all he could do was carry him to Africa. The Princess was delighted to see him again, but she was also sad to discover that she was the source of all their difficulty by leaving with the magnificent Light. However, Aladdin consoled her and told her he'd been dreaming of a way to bring it back. Aladdin left her mother. However, he returned soon with a strong sleeping dragon, and told her to accept the Magician with so-called goodness and spill it into his dinner wine that day to make him fall asleep so they should pull the Lamp out of him.

All went as they expected; the wine was consumed by the Magician, and when Aladdin walked in, he found himself falling asleep on the sofa. Aladdin pulled the Lamp out of his pocket, relying on the Genius to get the Castle, the Queen, and himself back to their home place.

The Sultan was as shocked and delighted at their return as he was distraught at his daughter's absence beyond compare.

As with Aladdin, he led long and prosperous lives with his lovely wife Bulbul, subsequently loving their good fortune.

2.6 Beauty and the Beast

There was once a prosperous businessman. He had three beautiful daughters but the most elegant was the smallest. Everybody named her Beauty when she was a girl and the name stuck with her through the years. Her sisters envied her because she was the brightest and kindest of the three, too.

When the ships sunk at sea, their father lost all of his capital. The family has had to move to a small village cottage. Each morning the man went to the fields to work, while each day Beauty did the cleaning and cooked lunch for her siblings. The only thing that her sisters did was to wake up late, roam about the whole day and lament they no longer had any beautiful clothes to wear.

A year went by. The father received a letter one day stating that one of the ships that he owned had returned unharmed. This meant the family was again prosperous.

The older sisters made a collection of items they needed their father to get for them after they read the story-suits, caps, shoes, earrings, bracelets and plenty more. "Don't you want me to get something for you too? "Beauty was questioned by her father. She felt the money they had wasn't going to be enough for the lists of her sisters, so she kindly responded, "If you ask, I want you to get me a rose, because there are no flowers in our house."

When the man finally reached the site where the ship was harbored, he found that the ship was in a pretty bad shape and it was also empty. Thus, the poor man got sad as he had to return home without any money and as a poor man. Only ten miles remaining to his house before a blizzard unexpectedly started. The snow was so heavy, and the winds were so strong that the man dropped twice off his horse.

It was evening and the guy felt he'd suffer from starvation and cold. Just then did he see a castle not far ahead? He got to the castle and got into a hall. There was a fire so he could dry out his clothing and arrange a table for one person only.

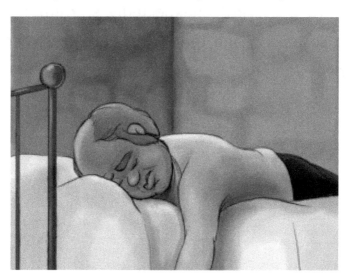

The guy waited to see if anybody would arrive, but when no one did, and he could no longer bear the hunger, he took the meal in front of him. He looked much healthier, and started enjoying the house. He eventually discovered a room practically set perfect for him. He didn't bother standing, he instead climbed in and promptly fell asleep.

He was amazed when he saw some clean clothes set out for him when he woke up the next day, instead of his own dirty clothes. He put them on, then went to find his horse outside. He went under an arch of roses on his way out of the house. He remembers her youngest daughter's demand of flower.

He plucked from the bush some flowers. He heard a hideous scream at once, and saw a beast charging for him. "So ungrateful you are! I offered you warmth, comfortable bed and clothes and you're still picking my flowers, the only thing I love really. Stay ready to go! "Please, sir, don't kill me," the guy answered, "I've got three lovely girls waiting for me to get home."

"I'm not your boss, I'm a beast, but don't flatter me. But you said you've got daughters. You should go, but you've got to guarantee that one of your daughters would come alone and die instead of you. If not, you'd have to come back and die in three months."

The beast then said something else which baffled the man. "I don't want you to leave the castle empty-handed. Take this bag before you depart and load it with as many gold and valuable stuff as you can carry."

He was feeling really bad. He brought Beauty the flowers which he had taken from the garden of the beast and told all what had happened. The older sisters began to sob but Beauty remained peaceful.

"Why don't you cry?" the sisters asked. "Father would die, only because of your crazy flowers." "Father won't die," she replied. "The beast asked father he should submit one of his daughters and so I'll go."

Nothing will alter her mind. The next day she departed with her father for the castle of the beast. On the road, her father told Beauty about the gold. She told her father to let her sisters use the money as a dowry...

Once they entered the palace they were confronted by the beast. "You have come here of your own will?" he questioned. "Indeed," said Beauty. "The heart is too sweet! "The beast roared, then ordered them to sleep well and eat food. "You may leave the palace tomorrow morning," the beast told the man.

Beauty started weeping the next morning, when her father left the palace. She assumed the beast would try to kill her. The child continued walking around the palace with her mind full of such horrible emotions. Everything was really attractive.

To her shock, she noticed a space that had a sign on it reading, "The Chambers of Beauty." The moment she opened the door her eyes stared at a lovely piano and library room. She thought that the beast did not want her to get bored. This gave the little girl courage and confidence. She desperately wanted to know about her family and how were they managing their life. The moment she thought about it the mirror on the wall displayed her home with family to her relief. She watched one of her sisters getting married. However, soon everything vanished. From this she figured out that probably the beast did not want to kill her.

She went into the dining room at dinner time. The beast was also sitting there. The beast asked her if he could watch her while she was having her meal. Beauty told him that she was comfortable with it and besides he was the master. The beast told her that she was the mistress of the castle and if she wanted, he could leave the room without any hesitation. The Beast asked her if she had found him ugly and horrible-looking.

Beauty couldn't lie so she said, "Yeah, I do, but I know you have a strong heart." "You are right. Not only am I horrible, I've absolutely no brains. I'm a beast, "he added, leaving her alone to have dinner.

The Beast entered the room at dinner time the next evening, and posed the Beauty a question that surprised her. "If I propose you then will you accept my offer? "He was wondering. "No, beast" she responded. He sighed again, and left the room. That's how they lived for three months-the life of Beauty would have been full if the beast didn't pose her one and the same question every night.

One day Beauty stood before the mirror, and saw her family again. She thought her dad was really sick. She went up to the beast and asked him what she had seen.

"I vowed never to abandon you, so I'm going to die from grief if you don't let me go," she told him. "You can go and see your relatives," he said, "but on the eighth day you have to guarantee you will be back. You will simply put your ring on the table when you are ready to come back.

"She woke up at her father's home the next morning. The father got very excited when he saw his youngest daughter healthy and well at home. His sisters came to see her, too. They were both very envious and furious that Beauty was all wrapped in a lovely dress and looked nicer than ever before.

They had devised a very wicked plan by which they wanted force the Beauty return to the castle later than she had promised in order to get the beast furious and slaughter her. When the eighth day arrived, they began to cry and to ask their youngest sister to live a little longer with them. The good heart of Beauty didn't even think that there could be a scheme because she felt that they really missed her. She vowed eight more days to live.

However, Beauty did have a dream on the tenth day. In her fantasy, the Beast lay almost dead in the garden. She woke up, and placed the ring on the table. She woke up in the Castle the next morning. She called for the beast but nobody replied.

Everywhere she looked for her Beast but was unable to locate him. She then recalled her dream and went out into the yard. She discovered the beast there. He'd fainted, however Beauty figured he'd demised. "He died for my sake! "She said, and a drop of tear dropped on his face.

Beast transformed into a beautiful prince as soon as Beauty's tears fell onto his face. Beauty was stunned. "I was turned by a fairy into a hideous beast long ago because when there was a hurricane, I didn't allow her shelter in the house," Beast clarified, "only seeking true love will break the spell. Are you going to marry me? "Beauty gladly accepted, and they stayed together at the castle for several long years.

Bedtime short Stories

"3 book of 10"

A Collection of Stories for Children to Relax and Sleep in Peace and Love

By Anna Smith

The trademarks that are used are without any consent and the publication of the trademark is without permission or backing by the trademark owner. All trademarks and brands within this book are for clarifying purposes only and are the owned by the owners themselves s, not affiliated with this document.

Chapter 1: Fictional Stories for kids

Fictional characters or things appear in novels, works, or movies only, and have never really occurred or happened. A fictional story is a kind of story written about fictitious characters and incidents that don't represent actual people or comply with the truth, or a fake claim or assertion you believe to be true:

1.1 Fur and Feather

The Pride and the Joy of mama Ostrich are her two newborn birds, her very own eggs hatched. One day, she stared and stared, as Mama Ostrich came home from having food for her two precious chicks. Yet nowhere will she locate her chicks! So-Oh god! What did she see on the field, except lion-tracks! Then just next to those tracks were the tracks of her two-foot chickens! Mama Ostrich, sad with anxiety, realized she needed to locate her children. And then she tracked signs of the lions. The footprints found their way through the forests and finished in a cave. Mama Ostrich walked into the cave's opening and gazed in. Her own precious chicks were there-in Mama Lion's embrace!

"What do you do to my chicks? "Mum, Ostrich screamed. "Bring them back to me instantly! "Why do you think about your chicks? "Mummy Lion's head raised and groaned. "Those are my cubs-it's plain to me! "It's just not simple to see," Mama Ostrich said. "There are chickens — oyster chickens — and I am an oyster, and you are a king! "What do you say to your chicks?" grumbled Mum Lion. "What is it? "With a snarl, Mama Lion said. "So you won't have any trouble locating some other species that will cooperate with you. I really warn you! Find some animal that's going to look me in the eye and tell me these are not my cubs. Repeat that, and I'm going to send it back to you. "Mama Lion lifted her large lion's head and screamed wild rust. Mom Ostrich took back easily to the bush. She has to say any animal she'd called a conference to speak about this awful crime. So-Oh god! What did she see on the field, except lion-tracks! Then just next to those tracks were the tracks of her two-foot chickens! Mama Ostrich, sad with anxiety, realized she needed to locate her children. And then she tracked signs of the lions. The footprints found their way through the forests and finished in a cave. Mama Ostrich walked into the cave's opening and gazed in. Her own precious chicks were there-in Mama Lion's embrace! "What do you do to my chicks? "Mum, Ostrich screamed. "Bring them back to me instantly! "Why do you think about your chicks? "Mummy Lion's head raised and groaned. "These are my cubs-it easy for me! "It's just not simple to see," Mama Ostrich said. "There are chickens — oyster chickens — and I am an oyster, and you are a king! "What do you say to your chicks?" grumbled Mum Lion. "What is it? "With a snarl, Mama Lion said. "So you won't have any trouble locating some other species that will cooperate with you. I really warn you! Find some animal that's going to look me in the eye and tell me these are not my cubs. Repeat it, and I'm going to send it back to you. "Mama Lion lifted her large lion's head and screamed wild rust. Mom Ostrich took back easily to the jungle. She has to say any animal she'd called a conference to speak about this awful crime. When she came to the Mongoose's den and told him her sad tale, Mongoose was thought and dreaming.

Suddenly, he had a notion. He said she was expected to go to an ant-hill deep inside the jungle. The ant-hill was higher than other species. She will dig an ant-hill crater in front of it. Then she would start searching until the pit behind the ant-hill comes back up. This was then that Mongoose had a notion. That was indeed an odd thing to say. "Why?" Mum Ostrich asked. "I am really tired," Mongoose said. "Listen." He said the depression needed to rise up behind the ant-hill, so no one was able to see it. She would say all the animals in the forests — and even Mama Lion — to come to that very ant-hill at sunset after she'd been finished digging the pit. And then Mama Ostrich went to the ant-hill, and the pit was filled. The same night, she went about asking all the animals to expect her there at sunset. She asked them how Mama Lion had taken away her nice, sweet chicks while all the animals were at the ant-hill. The zebras like antelopes, and all the other species, stared at Mama Lion's babies, then smiled. Mama Ostrich instructed the animals at sunset to come down to the ant-hill. Yet when Mama Ostrich claimed she wanted just one animal to look in the eye at Mama Lion and remind her she wasn't the chicks' mother, each and every animal in the meeting stared down at the table. Each beast, when questioned one by one, said in a gentle whisper that the little ones belonged to Mama Lion, and there was no doubt about that. He screamed as it came to Mongoose, "Have you ever seen a mum with a fur or feathered babies?

Only care about what you're doing! Mum, Lion's got hair! Chicks have feathers! We are members of an ostrich! "Then Mongoose hopped down the pit up against the ant-hill. Low, low the pit that he went to where the other end comes out, and he took back through the trees easily so anybody could see him moving. Once Mongoose leaped down the door, Mama Lion tried to leap after him, but he was too late. And the two ostrich chicks were released when Mama Lion went for Mongoose! Obviously, they raced straight into the open arms of their mother. "Think about what you're doing! Mama Lion has hair!" Mama Lion paced and paced by the ant-hill opening, not aware of the trap behind the ant-hill. The other creatures at the conference backed forward, one by one, very carefully and with caution. And for a very, very long time, Mama Lion was left standing in front of the ant-hill.

1.2 Prince and a Snake

The Vijaygarh Empire had a wise and generous Queen. People were grateful. Yet the King himself was concerned and depressed. A devilish snake had gotten into the body of his friend. Neither medicine nor magic healed his family. When the Prince grew up, he figured, "It is because of me that my father was concerned." So one day, he fled the castle. Traveling, he came to another country. He discovered a lonely temple, so he started to stay there. He asked for food.

The King of that country was cruel, but he had a lovely and beautiful daughter. The King became disappointed with his family. To the barren city, the Prince and his new wife set off. They paused on their way to take some break. The Princess wandered about searching for food, as her husband went to sleep. As the Princess returned, she was surprised to find a snake lying on the mouth of her friend. Another snake perched on a neighboring shelf. They talked between themselves. "Why don't you leave the Prince's body? He's so sweet and nice, "said the snake sitting on the mound." You're bad too! You're threatening passers-by; you shouldn't tell me what to do, "answered the snake was sitting on the Prince's head. Using all her bravery, the Princess destroyed both of the snakes. He told him of the two snakes as her husband awaked. The Prince was pleased. Instead, he'd asked her who he was. We proceeded to the residence of the King. The King rejoiced to see his family. When the King heard of the death of the devilish serpent, his happiness knew no bounds. Together with life together with the Prince and the Queen. The Kingdom marked the day after a few years, during which the Royal couple gave birth to one boy and one girl children.

1.3 The Mermaid (A fairy tale)

Once In Scotland, a young man was so in love with lass that he had done little but dreamed about her day and night. Finally, he had the confidence to give her his heart and, in exchange, asked for hers. But as it may happen, she did not express the same emotion. She grinned sweetly at him and then walked ahead. It left the young man feeling depressed and defeated. The youth was full of shame. He realized like he couldn't show his face around town anymore. Not everybody realizes that she'd handed him up! With his mates at the beach, he couldn't even catch anymore, because he was so full of guilt. So he gathered his nets with a heavy heart, climbed into his boat and headed off to a desolate island. He constructed himself a cabin, and sailed to sea every morning, quite early. He'd throw his nets there and potentially haul in a day's catch. He brought his catch to the port nearest to the shore, where nobody recognized his name. He'd sell his fish to the local market, buy food and other needs with the money he'd won, and sail back to his island. That was his work, day in and day out. And one day, something gleamed at the corner of his eye, with the fish in his jar. Quickly, though it struggled and thrashed, he caught it with one fist and wrapped the net into a knot so that whatever it was could not flee. "Let me just go! "He heard a screaming voice. She was a mermaid, to his horror! She appeared like any other person from the waist up, but a thick fishtail that glittered with glossy yellow-green scales flipped underneath. "A sires! "And he told. "You know as well as I do you have to give me a wish." "Oh good," the mermaid replied, "I suppose you want a bag of gold coins. I happen to learn with these riches of a sunken ship not far from here." "I am not involved in coins, "he said. "'That won't give me what I want." "So it's a treasure trunk that you need? "With dignity, she turned her back. "I'm the King of the Sea's aunt, so I can get my servants to bring such a trunk to your island." "If you care enough about me to ask about my island," he said, "you care what I really want." "Seer maid sighed. "Why did she? "Ooh, why do you ask? "And he told. "Blue hair. Her color is light white. The direction that she's going. She is everything I desire desperately from all over the country. I don't want anything else than I can't get her! "Ah, she is not that unique," the mermaid said. But when the young man tightened his hold

on the netting, she mimed irately said, "I may, of course, grant your love wish, but you have to know it takes some time. Release me, and I'll ring a magic bell for you. When you go to her and sell her the ring after a year and a day, she won't decline." "How do you think she won't get married by then? "She won't be," the mermaid said. And he wanted to set free the mermaid. He took the key and placed it on his nightstand in a pot. He wanted to mark the wood on the mantelpiece to keep a note of the passage of daily life. Not long after that, one day, when he was heading back to his island, he noticed what looked like a mass of seaweed. Even more interesting was when the seaweed passed. He then realized it wasn't a pile of seaweed, but a brown-haired teenager whose black hair lay round her in a heap. "What do you do at my place, here? "He was frowning.

"Ooh, 'this is not your paradise, only because you first came here,' she said. "You're not the only person who has needed to go everywhere! My dad's got a new wife, not that long older than me. She's terrible and evil, and I'm scared she'll do something bad to me." "You can't stay here. You have to go back to make things right with her. "She replied," It is not up to you to advise me what to do. "Apart from that, I cannot go out right now because the winds are not perfect." "The winds will shift tomorrow morning." "And my canoe is destroyed." "I'll repair it." "Stop it! I have to remain where I'm, alone and free! "I do it! "The young man thundered." You're going to have plenty of space, "she said. "You're living on your island side, and I'm living on mine. Besides, "she said more softly," if I prepare for myself, I can eat plenty for two as well. "Subscribe," he said. "But I eat by myself." The girl was true to her word. When the young man came back from fishing or from the market, he would notice a hot meal on the table for him. He did not know where she went, where she worked, and at the least, he did not ask. He'd had a really nice day that day. The fish were available and were having a reasonable price on the market. He got home sooner than normal, noticing the girl in his room. She was stunned and decided to leave. He said, "You don't have to ride too hard out there now. Take a plate and lie down opposite me. We could eat together, as well. "So they ate together, so they said nothing. But when he came back the next day she was there too, so when they ate together they spoke a couple more words. The next day, a couple more terms, before they got to learn more about each other. He completely understood that the girl needed to flee her home, so when she told him about her father and how oblivious he was to the risky position he needed to put her in, he pounded the table with indignation. She listened sympathetically to the story of his lost love, and how, after the 365 days, he hoped to capture her heart with the ring of the mermaid. She also put a map over the mantle to keep track of the days that had passed past and those remaining. He figured it was a smart plan since the marks on the wood had been difficult to say apart and to hold count. Not long after that, one day, the young man came home from fishing and found she had carried flowers out of the field and planted them in front of the house. "How beautiful and compassionate," he asked himself. She is starting helping him docks the boat at that point, extending the nets. While she was just a little brown-haired girl who was almost as small as a boy, she was remarkably powerful and helpful to have around. The girl said one morning, "When you go to the store, you have to carry back some window glass to keep the weather out." He pushed, and the next day, when he was away, she inserted the glass in the window holes. Indeed that evening, the hut remained colder. And through the fresh opening, a ray of sunshine shone through the day. She asked him another time, "Bring me back some white paint-these walls are just too dreary." He replied, and she washed the walls, painting them white. He had to admit that his hut was cozier than ever before, though he continued to grumble over what little money was left after he had fetched her this or fetched her that. One day, on the other side of the island, he found a mound of grass being forced against a group of dense trees and being squeezed down into the center. He knew it had to be where she was staying at night. A bit shamed that he had never thought about it before, he resolved to forego fishing for a couple of days and started cutting wood and hammering it into the shelter. "Who are you so far? "She was wondering. "'It does not fit for a young woman to sleep on a mound of grass outside,' he said. "This will be your own place," she sniffed. "Don't do it on my page." "I'm just right where I'm." However, when she paced around the house that evening, he realized that she was humming to herself. A song close to one that his mother used to play. And then the days easily past. It was the 365th day until he realized it, a whole year after he found the mermaid in his net on a fateful day. As the lad reached the hut that afternoon, he saw the girl with the magic ring on her finger in front of the hearth, keeping up her hand and gazing at it from any perspective. "What is it you are doing? "He's barking. "Nothing," she immediately replied, lowering the ring back into the container and covering it with the cap. "Just make sure tomorrow's ring is nice for anything." Then she went to her place. She kept a fabric bag with all her things upon returning. "I'm going now. I'm going back home to my brother." "What? Aren't you nervous about how they're going to handle you? "I'm going to handle it. "One year is enough." "Oh ... the winds aren't perfect." "They'll be early." "Sorry, we never patched your raft. I'm going to give you a cruise ride." "I had the graft repaired. I will only quit as soon as I came if that's all right with you. "She went over to the map, pulled it off the board, put it in front of him, and listed the last day off. "Tomorrow," she said, "you will assert your true love for yourself." And she left. The juvenile sat in his chair for the remainder of the day. He looked at the floor and the ground. He fell asleep in the chair. When he woke up early the next morning, the first thing he noticed was the map before him on the bed. He went over to the mantle, where he kept the ring of the mermaid and set off to pursue his life's love. Just he wasn't born into the village where he put his boat. It was to the girl's land that had lived on the island with him. To see him invade the garden of her aunt, you can imagine how shocked she was. "Oh, my goodness! I didn't dream of seeing you here, "he said." Well, I am here. "You find the love of your life, then?" Yeah, I did that. I say I have now." "So she's going to get you? "The girl questioned, looking at the ring he was carrying opposite her. "Tell me," he said, and then stared into her eyes. "Oh, she may," the girl said. "How about if to make comfortable you and the girl owe it a bit of time? "And one grinned at another. They've earned their breath, everything they do. The young man found a spot not far from her and regularly went fishing. They were getting dinner at night, so they spoke and spoke. They feel more confident every day than the previous day. And then the two were wedded, and it was a lovely ceremony, with all the relatives and friends that the girl and boy felt they were crossed with, but that they were no longer mad. If something they'd ever been made. And then the young man and his dark-haired wife lived the remainder of their days living happily.

1.4 A Dangerous Helper and the Forest

There was the lake in thick woodland. Both the creatures had been consuming water from the pool. This lake's water was so good that, for a long time, many fish stayed there. A crab had originated in this area. The closest mate of the crabs was a swan. The swan had been at the same pool. They had been content in each other's business. Their joy continued until a snake found its home by the lake one day. The swan laid an egg every single day . The snake will come and make it swallowed away. "I have to find a way to save my eggs," the swan thought. Every day, he went to the crab and said, "Please save me, my friend. My eggs are under attack. The

evil snake consumes all the eggs in the nest. The crab was sitting for a moment. Instead, he said: "I've got an idea. Let's capture some fish from this lake and spread them from the house of the snake to the house of the mongoose. "A mongoose stayed in the surrounding forest. So the crab and the swan caught some fish and dumped them from the house of the mongoose to the house of the snake. Instead, they all hid behind a forest and observed. They waited for some time. He consumed them all one by one, happily. While he fed, he managed to track the fish path to the house of the lizard. The mongoose eventually entered the Snake's room. All the crab and the swan observed all these happenings sitting behind the stone. After seeing the mongoose, the snake figured, "The mongoose is here to strike me. I have a great war for it. "For some time, the snake started to clash with the mongoose. They battled for some time. In a heated struggle, the mongoose destroyed the snake. Seeing this behind the vine, the swan and the crab raised a breath of satisfaction, but their happiness was short-lived. They agreed after a few days to shape yet another strategy to get rid of the harmful buddy-mongoose. It has to be careful when battling an opponent.

1.5 A Tree who was Ugly

Long, years ago, thousands of large, majestic trees stood in thick woodland. They were content but, despite themselves, confident. There was even one hideous tree among them whose roots were poorly twisted. Its origins consisted of irregular curve s. All the plants were making fun with the

hideous guy. "What did you think, hunchback? "The other trees still yelled, and their laughing made the ugly tree feel bad. Yet, he never raised a voice towards them. The ugly tree said," I wish I were as pretty as the other trees. Why did God do this to me? Neither will I offer shelter to the travelers so the birds cannot build their nests on me. No one wants me. He looked at the trees and said, "These trees are magnificent. I have to kill them." As soon as he picked up his chain, the trees were afraid. 'Chop, Chop, Chop' went down the woodcutter's chain, and one by one, the trees started to collapse. "None of us can be saved," one of the lovely trees yelled. Fast the woodcutter's hammer took the tree to the ground too. The woodcutter had by now come near to the hideous oak. He had just lifted his hammer when he immediately realized the hideous tree was crooked. "Mm! This crooked tree strikes me as useless. I can't create long straight logs with this hideous tree, "he said. And he shifted towards another beautiful tree. The hideous tree raised a massive sigh of relief. He knew that by rendering him ugly, Nature had really offered him a gift. From that day, the ugly tree never protested. He was content despite his crooked limbs.

The End

1.6 Forest and a Caterpillar

ONE Good DAY, Caterpillar stepped out and came to a hole. "My, Oh god! "Caterpillar said. "It is a really pretty place! "Caterpillar was staring at the cave entrance. "I see nothing in there," he added. "I'm moving home." Caterpillar had gone back. And then on top of a mountain, Caterpillar inched in. And it was there that he fell asleep. Just at the same moment, Hare, who stayed in that cave, was out for a stroll, too. She'd noticed signs on the field as Hare returned home.

This awoken Caterpillar. Then in a really strong voice, Caterpillar boomed, "It is I! Yeah, I who's stamping rhinos in the soil and turning elephants into ashes! "Hare was hopping with terror. "What would a tiny thing like me do against a beast that is stamping rhinos and elephants? "Jackal went by easily. Hare replied, "Brother Jackal, someone has fallen into my cellar! Can you support me, please? "Jackal replied," Yeah, I'm glad to assist. "Jackal went up into the cave and aggressively barked," Whish's in my friend's room, Hare? "With an accent that shook the world, Caterpillar cried out. "It is me! Indeed, I who in the world stamps rhinos and drives elephants into ashes! "Jackal thought in terror on learning this," I can do nothing about such a monster! "Then, as soon as he could, Jackal took off. Leopard then walked by. Hare had told Leopard everything that has happened. Leopard replied, "I'm stronger than Jackal, and I'm smaller." Leopard screamed at the door of the cave, "Who's in my buddy Hare's house? "The same way Caterpillar called back he had done before. Leopard was astounded. He said, "When rhinos and elephants are marked by this guy, I don't even want to worry about what he might do to me! "So Leopard immediately took back. It came to Rhino. "Everyone knows how large and distressing I am," Rhino grunted. He marched back into the cave of Hare. He snorted and paddled his really large feet to the deck. Yet when Rhino asked who was inside the cave, and heard the roaring response from Caterpillar, he said, "This is not nice! Would he get me carved into the earth? I'm from here! "Then Rhino sped backward, smashing into the jungle. "They're outta here! "And Rhino flew away, running into the jungle." Only Elephant wanted to assist. Yet, like the rest, as Elephant learned what Caterpillar had to say, he realized he had no urge to be riddled like ashes. So he walked away very fast, too. Hare didn't know what to do! So Frog went by. "What's wrong?" Frog asked, and then Hare said to him. "Maybe I should save you," Frog said. "I wish you could," Frog said. "You're so tiny!" "You can't help!" said Rhino. Both the animals chuckled. "He needs to," said Hare. "Why not have Frog try?" Then Frog went to the cave door and questioned who was inside. He got the same reaction that the others did. The frog then went closer and yelled, "I, who am the toughest of all, have actually come. I'm the one that stamps the rhinos!

The End.

1.7 Death of a Man Eater

Tigers consume the meat of many wild creatures. Tigers usually don't kill tigers. They do enjoy the meat of other creatures. In capturing other animals, a tiger needs to be really quick. Yet an elderly tiger cannot move far, or a wounded tiger. You will just attract us in moments such as such. People are not permitted to move as quickly as

animals. While tigers or other species are easy targets. A tiger does not have some more food despite having consumed human meat already. That kind of tiger is considered a man-eater. A tiger once transformed a man-eater in a forest in Uttar Pradesh, India. In the forest, she had murdered both women and people. Such people went through the forests to harvest firewood, vegetables, roots, and other items. Citizens have avoided moving into the forest following these act indents. Instead, the man-eater made much-repeated trips to the local villages. It destroyed humans or domestic animals. The villagers got panicky. The authorities concerned decided to do more about it. It called on Jim Corbett to assist the villagers. He also promised to hunt the man-eater down. Jim Corbett was a professional shooter. He had gained a great deal of familiarity with tigers and other wildlife. He became a nature enthusiast. He didn't like shooting wild creatures for entertainment or fun. Yet he had no interest in attacking man-eaters. It was just about supporting depressed men. Jim Corbett and his rifle entered the settlement. The gun was a good one. It could kill massive and influential animals like lions, tigers, and elephants. He had collected all the details regarding the man-eater. He picked a spot. The tiger has always come there. The network was designed by Jim Corbett. This platform has been set to a division big. Tied to the nearest tree was a small buffalo. Jim Corbett had been waiting all night. Yet there was no tiger going. Perhaps the hidden man and his powerful one had scented it. Jim Corbett reversed his strategy. He re-entered the town. Next came the bear. Buffalo was defeated. And, in the forest, it pulled dead buffalo. The villagers conveyed this news to Jim Corbett. In pursuit of the tiger, Jim Corbett then went into the wood. He'd eventually reached the location. He scaled a tree to figure out what the tiger was. The tiger had taken a meal of the buffalo's dead flesh. From a point, he was pretending. He approached the road gradually and with care. Upon a decent meal, he observed the tiger lying back. He paused on, killing a sleeping tiger at first. But that was not a healthy tiger then. We became a man-eater. With that thought in mind, he put two bullets into the head of the sleeping tiger. The tiger died suddenly. The villagers were pleased.

With his courage, Jim Corbett has been praised.

The End

1.8 Puma and a Spanish Girl

Once the Spaniards invaded South America five hundred years ago, the Indigenous American people also struck hard against the settlers. One way for the Spanish tribes to bring pressure was to surround their villages. This is what occurred in the early 1500s when a Spanish girl called Maldonado was 15 years old. Hostile Querandí Native Americans had invaded the Spanish village where Maldonado stayed. The food stocks became exhausted

before long. Citizens were suffering famine. They pleaded their captain to let them take their chances to flee the settlement in search of food- but that would not make the

captain. Hungry, Maldonado ran from the village and fled into the forest. When the night falls, she heard the calling of wild animals with fear. Where could she have a good night's sleep? However, there was one call that drew her closer. This was a painful sound. She tracked the echo to a grotto where she met a puma that had just arrived. Maldonado helped cleanse the cubs from the mother's puma. Later, when the mother went out to hunt, her s tarred at the children. And then the days past. One day, when Maldonado gathered food, and the mother puma and her cubs were inside the cave, Querandí warriors shocked the child. They caught her and moved her to their village. Fearing the worst, Maldonado braced herself for her demise, which she was confident was imminent. Yet the Girl was kind to the Querandís. In their community, they gave her tasks to help, and she gladly took part. One day, a band of Spaniards invaded the village of Querandí. Recognizing a Spanish child, Maldonado was caught and pushed back to her house. The Spanish captain became angry that by fleeing to the forest, she had disobeyed Him. To give her an illustration, he ordered her to be bound to a tree and left there to devour wild animals. After many days, ventured the unhappy villagers where Maldonado had been bound to the vine, expecting the worst. They find her tightly bound to the tree and very much alive, much to their shock. We were even more shocked to discover that it was a mother puma that had cooked and sheltered the girl all this time.

The End

1.9 The King and his Palace

A King stayed in there thousands of years ago. His citizens liked him because he worked well with their desires. He will invite several noblemen of his Realm at the end of each month to examine his job and offer him advice. The King designed loads of things. He'd restore his palace every year, and every time it looked better than before. "Superb! Unbeatable!! One day the King said, "This year I should  create the perfect palace with all the comforts. It will be celebrated not just inside my realm but also by the citizens of the surrounding states." On the next day, the King figured out the best plan for his best palace. He turned it off to the designers and masons until it was finalized. In around a month, the King's ideal dream palace was finished. The King has welcomed his kingdom's officials, as well as surrounding nations, to get their views on the building. "Incredible! Indeed, it's a beautiful palace, "the nobles applauded in agreement, but a saint standing in the corner was quiet. The King asked why the saint was quiet as everybody celebrated his palace. He went up to the saint and said," Please tell me, O Saint, why are you silent? Isn't my palace great? "The saint replied with a gentle voice," Dear King! Your palace is reinforced and will last forever. It's lovely but not ideal because it's people who reside in it. They are not permanent. Your house will exist indefinitely, but the men in it will not survive. Therefore I'm deaf. Man is born with empty hands, and so is he who dies. "The King praised the saint for his wise advice and once again sought to create a grand palace.

The End

1.10 A Girl and her Beautiful hair

There once lived a merchant who sold perfumes in a city called Hindustan, and he had a daughter named Dorani whom he loved dearly. Dorani had a fairy friend, and both Dorani and her fairy friend could sing more sweetly and dance more gracefully than anyone else in the kingdom. For this cause, the ruler, or rajah, of the fairyland kept them in high regard. And the name of the rajah was Indra. Dorani has the world's loveliest beauty, for it was like the gold ground, and its scent was like the fragrance of fresh flowers. But her hair was so long and heavy that it was always intolerable in weight. She chopped off a gleaming tress one day. Wrapping her hair in a wide vine, she flung it down into the water flowing right beneath her bed. And it came to pass that the king's son was hunting away, and had gone down to the river to drink when a folded leaf from which came a scent of roses drifted toward him. He opened it, and within, he noticed a hair lock like spinning gold, from which a small, exquisite scent emerged. He seemed so depressed and so silent when the prince returned home that day that his father worried if something evil had befallen him, and told his son what the matter was. The youth took the hair tress that he'd noticed in the water. Holding it up to the sun, he responded, "Look, my lord, was there ever hair like this? If I can gain and

marry the maiden who owns that hair lock, I will die!" And the king quickly sent heralds through all his dominions to look for the damsel with hair like spun gold. He eventually discovered that she was the perfume merchant's girlfriend. Rumor is growing exponentially. Soon Dorani also learned about this. She said to her father, "If the hair is mine, and the king wants me to marry his son, then I will do so. But please ask the king to allow me this: that after the wedding, while I can stay in the palace all day, I wish to return to my old home every night." Her father listened to her with amazement but replied nothing because he realized she was wiser than he. The hair was Dorani's, of course, and the king soon summoned the perfume dealer, informing him that he required his daughter to be offered to the prince in marriage. The dad lowered his head to the ground three times. He answered, "Your highness is our lord, and we will do whatever you want us to do. The maiden requests only this- that if, after the wedding, she remains at the palace all day that she should be able to return to her father's house at night." The king thought this was a very odd order, but said to himself that it was, after all, the business of his wife and the girl will certainly tire of going back and forth early. So he did not cause any noise, and it was done easily, and the wedding was celebrated with great rejoicing. At first, the situation attached with the lovely Dorani to his wedding bothered the prince very little, for he figured he should at least see his wife during the daytime. But to his dismay, he realized that she was going to do nothing but stay on a stool all the time, bowing her head over her feet, and he could never convince her to utter a sound. Each evening she was brought back to her house on a raised frame, borne on poles on four men's backs, a vehicle named a palanquin. Shortly after daybreak, Dorani returned that morning; but never a sound passed her lips, nor did she give her husband by any indication during the day that she saw, heard, or heeded. Unhappy and depressed, as he came across the old gardener, who had worked the prince's great grandparents, the prince walked in an ancient and magnificent garden outside the palace. When the old gardener saw the child, he came and bowed before him and asked, "Boy, why do you look so sad, what's the matter?" The child answered, "I'm sad, old friend, because I've married a wife as lovely as the stars, yet she won't talk to me a single thing, and I don't know what to do. He returned a little later with five or six tiny packets, which he put in the hands of the young man. He said, "Today, as your bride leaves the house, spray the powder over your body from one of those packages. When you keep seeing it plainly yourself, you'll become transparent to everybody else. I can't do much, so maybe it's all going well for you!" The prince praised him and gently placed the packages away in his turban. After Dorani left for her father's house the next night, the prince sprayed the magic powder on himself, and then rushed after her. He was still unseen to all else, but he looked as ordinary and was able to perceive everything that came before him. He easily grabbed the palanquin and marched next to it to the dwelling of the perfume merchant. His wife moves into the house nearby. He stood behind her, quietly. Dorani progressed to her own room where two huge basins were mounted, one filled with the scent of rose oil and one of water. She washed in these, and then arrayed herself in a silver gown, wounded pearl strings around her waist, while her head was topped with a wreath of roses. She sat down on a four-legged stool over which was a canopy of silken curtains while fully clothed. She painted these round her. She then cried out, "Fly, stool, go!" The stool went up in the air immediately. The invisible prince, who had watched all these proceedings with great wonder, seized it by one leg as it flew away, and found himself being borne through the air at a rapid rate. They arrived in a short time at the house of Dorani's fairy buddy, who was also a favorite of the ruler, or rajah, of the fairyland, as I told you before. The fairy stood waiting on the threshold, as beautifully dressed as Dorani herself was. As the stool landed at her entrance, the fairy friend exclaimed in astonishment, "Oh, the stool is flying all crooked today! I believe you've been talking to your boyfriend, so it won't fly straight." Yet Dorani announced that she hadn't said one word to him, and she couldn't imagine why the stool was flying like leaning down on one side. The fairy looked uncertain, but gave no response, and took her seat next to Dorani, the prince keeping one leg closely again. The stool then kept on all across the air until it entered Indra the rajah's palace. The woman sang and danced before the rajah Indra during the night, while a mystical lute played the most enchanting music the prince had ever heard, and the prince became very entranced. The rajah gave the signal to cease just before dawn. Again the two women sat on the stool and flew back to earth with the prince holding to one hip and safely carried Dorani and her husband to the merchant's perfume store. The prince dashed straight on to the palace here. When he crossed his own space threshold, he was noticeable once more. He then laid down on a couch and waited for the arrival of Dorani. She took a seat as soon as she arrived, and remained as quiet as possible, bowing her head on her knees. Not a sound was detected for a time. The prince said now, "I dreamed a strange dream last night, and as it was all about you, I'm going to tell you, even though you're not listening to something." The kid, in truth, didn't react to his words and stayed as ever before. But despite that, he went on to describe every single event he had seen the previous evening, leaving no information. And when he lauded her singing-and, his voice shook a little bit-Dorani just stared at him, but she said naught, though she was packed with wonder in her own eyes. "What a sight!" she penned. "Could it have been a dream? How could he have learned what I've achieved in a dream? "Nevertheless, she remained still. Just once, she glanced at the prince, and then spent the entire day as before, bowing her head on her knees. As night arrived, the prince again made her invisible and pursued her. The same thing occurred again as before, but Dorani has sung better than ever. "I was there," the prince replied. "So why are you trailing me? "And the girl said, 'Why,' replied the boy, 'I love you, and to be with you is happiness.' This time Dorani's eyelids trembled, so she said no more, and remained quiet the rest of the day. Then at night, when she climbed into her palanquin, she said to the prince, 'If you love me, show it by not accompanying me tonight.' So the boy did when she wanted, and he stayed at home. You had to converse with your friend! "And Dorani replied, 'Yes, I did talk! "Yet she wouldn't say it anymore. That night Dorani has sung so beautifully that at the end of the day, the rajah Indra stood up and promised that she should inquire whatever she wanted and give it to her. At first, she was quiet, but when he questioned her, she replied," If you agree, then I'm asking for the magic flute. "The rajah, knowing this, was frustrated with himself for having such a pledge, because he's going to go. Dorani bent her head softly as she took the lute. She went with the fairy from the great gate where the stool was waiting for them. More fragile than ever, it fell down to earth. Every morning, as Dorani returned to the palace, she told the prince if he had ever wished before. He smiled in joy, for this time she had talked to him of her own free will. "She stood up and flung herself into his arms and said," Never again! Nay, I will never abandon you again! "So the prince received his lovely bride. Even while none of them struggled with the fairies even their power anymore, they heard more every day about the beauty of love that one can always know, even if the power of the fairy has long ago departed.

The End.

1.11 A Wealthy Merchant and the Fragrance

A rich businessman had settled in a small town. He was really generous and kind. He had a friend, who unfortunately fell into a poor business. The merchant had told his son several times not to go with the poor business. Yet all of this in vain. "Please, don't tell me what to do, father. I know what's right for me, and I know what to do, "said the son. One day, a great saint came to the area. The merchant went to the saint, prayed for his blessings, and said," My rich son is the only cause of my concern. Please support me. "After a few minutes of meditation, the saint said," Send your son to my Ashram tomorrow morning. I will talk to him. "Next morning, the merchant sent his son to the saint's Ashram. There the saint told the son to pluck a rose-flower from the Ashram's garden. The son did as the saint ha d requested. Then the saint told the son," Smell it and enjoy its scent, my

boy. "Then the saint gave the boy a wheat sack and said," Hold the rose near to the bag. The saint told the boy back after an hour to sample the rose again. "What is it feeling right now? "The saint told the child, and the child smelled the rose and replied, 'It smells as fine as before.' The saint then said, 'Hmm! Then hold the rose close to this jiggery bag. "The boy did so. After an hour, the saint told the boy again to feel the rose." Is there any difference in the fragrance? "The saint told the child. "No. No. Everything smells as new as ever, "answered the child. And the saint said," Son, you want to be like this rose, give others a scent while at the same time not letting someone put the poor smell on you. Your positive qualities are your power. You need not sacrifice them in bad business. "I am thankful to you, O Father, for raising my heart," said the son of the businessman. From that day forward, he was sincere and generous, like his father, who was a learned man.

The End

1.12 Golden Arrow and the Robin Hood

No man in the entire world was greater than Robin Hood with a bow and arrow. He stayed in Sherwood Park, with his Merry Men team. It was the forests where the King kept his royal herd. King Richard had controlled the territory several years ago. King Richard let disadvantaged men reach Sherwood Forest. They were able to kill the deer and provide food for their kin. Yet the time had come to abandon England for King Richard and his Force. His younger brother John took up the throne, as long as he was finished. Poor King John does not allow anybody to chase the royal deer into Sherwood Forest. Everyone caught shooting the King's deer in Sherwood Forest will be thrown in prison from then on! One thing that Robin Hood didn't like. He fled into woodland in Sherwood. Dressed in green from his helmet to his pants, Sherwood Forest trees were able to cover him while he was chasing the King's deer. Some courageous people come to Sherwood Forest on occasion. They followed Robin Hood one after the other and became his Merry Men. As wealthy knights and dukes went into the forests, Robin Hood and his Merry Men would conceal themselves. They'd then just run out at once to steal some rich guys. Robin Hood should give poor people the capital. The affluent people who were robbed

were not satisfied. We asked Bad King John what hap had penned at Sherwood Forest. "There needs to be something said about that!" they said. The King took over the Sheriff of Nottingham from Sherwood Forest. Catching Robin Hood will be his work-once and for all! Yet the man was too fast in gold. His Merry Men will alert him any time they saw Nottingham's Sheriff or one of his guards in the forests. So, a fresh idea came about with the Sheriff. "I'm trying to call for a major contest," he said, "to find out who with a bow and arrow is strongest in the country. The winner will go home with a Golden Arrow. "In a quiet voice, the Sheriff said," If I know Robin Hood, he won't be able to keep away from such a contest. So we'll spot him as he arrives! "Don't go to the draw, Robin Hood! "Little John said. Robin Hood most liked Little John of all the Merry People. "It is a trick! "And he told. "When they catch you, they're out to kill you." Robin Hood said nothing. He just decided to fly. Ten great bowmen lined up on contest day. The circular goal was too far out. The black and red circles were hard to see. Each young man fired his strongest gun, one at a time. Any of the arrows fell on goal. None came near the middle. One of his guards was handed to the Sheriff. "Were you staring at him? Is he here? "Sire, no. Robin Hood possesses crimson eyes. None of those snipers have red ears." "The wimp! "The sheriff said. "He's scaring me! This is why he remained down. "There were two bowmen then. The first became William, the guy of the Sheriff. William took aim with caution. His arrow fell right in the center of the goal-a bull's eye! William got support from the audience. It was time for the most current bowman. His arrow had also flown across the sea. This fell right into the blade of the eye of William's bull and sliced it in two! The bowman would let go of two more arrows in a moment. Each flew to where the Sheriff was seated, pinning him to his position, with one arrow on either leg. The Sheriff didn't realize what had happened! The guy in green then took a black wig off and dropped it to the table. "Take him back, you sheriff Screamed. "Robin Hood! "But our hero hopped up a horse over the wall waiting for him. He's done! He just ran! This story is one of Robin Hood's numerous exploits, the most beloved character in England. And one of the most loved heroes in the world.

The End

1.13 John Smith and a Pocahontas (A Folk Tale)

Three ships arrived on the coast of what is America today, in the spring of 1607. Approximately 100 people – no women were invited to join – walked into the sand to begin a new existence. The people designed twenty cabins, and a fort to go all over. They named Jamestown as their new place. However, they were not the only people living on that property. Tribes of Native Americans existed up and down the coast and for miles into the forests. The area is named Virginia today. This used to be renamed the Powhatan Confederacy back then. In the Powhatan Confederacy, more than 30 tribes were governed by one chief. Powhatan was modeled for him. The scouts from Chief Powhatan informed him new people had landed at the beach. They told him they had built a fort for the men. They also informed him that the young people were communicating in terms that none had learned before. We were sporting clothing that nobody had seen before. Powhatan was mindful of all this. What he didn't ask-and most of all, what he needed to know was, where did they come from? Why did they stay here? So what will their Manager look like? However, they were not the only people living on that property. His scouts even told him some other news, which was quite strange. Several seeds were cultivated throughout the fortress. There were no canoes around the fort anywhere, so the people did not even stop for fishing by the water. The people did not go fishing in the forests, however. Powhatan said, "These people have no idea how to cultivate, ride a boat, fish or hunt. This would be better than their President, I thought. We're going to carry them vegetables-maize, beans, and squash. They're going to dry out without us. And I, Powhatan, who rules 30 nations, will still reign over them! "Let me come with you, Dad! "The daughter of Powhatan, Pocahontas, wrote. No-one noticed her disappear into the longhouse. "I do want to see the building." "Of course not! "His father said. "You need to do the job here. You should play with your sisters when you're finished." "I, Pohawtan, who rules 30 tribes, can rule over them too! "Every day, I play with them! "Pocahontas said. "Thanks, Father! I am going to be fine! "Powhatan screamed.

"OH, my love," he said. "How do I say no to this face? "A Pocahontas story, at last! She was sure she might explode if she had to tie beads onto another moccasin or fill one more basket with berries! And Chief Powhatan, with scouts bearing maize, rice, with squash baskets with Pocahontas behind them, went all over to the castle. Once they arrived there, the baskets calmed down. Then withdrew. With huge smiles on their faces, people burst out of the fort in a minute. You can be confident there was a lot of fun! Pocahontas

noticed something important as well that made her happy. The other people came out with four boys a little older than her. She grinned at the people.

They waived back! As the grown-ups wanted to speak to each other with their arms and legs, she asked them, "Will you like to play? "People erupted with big smiles on their faces from the building. We didn't get what she was doing. But then they taught her how to play stickball and tag. Then she taught them how to perform those cartwheels. Powhatan, after a moment, cried out, "Pocahontas! It is time to leave. "Pocahontas returned to the fort about four to five days after that, like the others. Powhatan's scouts were bringing maize, cabbage, and beans each day. Maple sugar even often for a sweet treat. Pocahontas heard her best mates' names-John, Nathaniel, Henry, and Samuel. And hers, they heard. She learned their leader's name, John Smith, too. The rain started falling, as the days were shorter. The maize had dried up in the area. The squash and the vineyard beans dried up. Beans, drying up on the trees. "We will no longer carry food to the City," Powhatan said. "We need to conserve all that we can so that our people can make it through the winter. We need to go to the fort and inform them. "Powhatan said," We will no longer carry food to the fort. When the people learned the news in the fort, they became furious. They were marching into cabins. For weapons, they came out and fired the cannons in the room. Powhatan, too, was angry. He said, "O white people, I advise you! Do not go past our village to anywhere! If you did, then you'll be sorry! "Jamestown's people were unwilling to grasp what Powhatan said. But from his profile, they could see they were no longer friends. Shortly after that, John Smith entered the woods in pursuit of fruit. He'd been next to Powhatan village. O close. He was seen walking by Powhatan's brother and another family. They'd run at him in a blur. They tied down John Smith and then carried him back to the town of Powhatan. "We'll kill that now, once and for all," Powhatan added. "I'm going to be the Captain of all the men at the castle. "Nobody goes past our town! If you did, then you'll be sorry! "Yohn Smith was forced to escape the village that year. Today, it helped Powhatan feel at home. Pocahontas, who had met him since the beginning, spent time with him. Day after day, they'd show each other the terms the people said to each other. When the snow fell, the residents of the town of Powhatan began getting ready for a celebration. In his longhouse, Powhatan named John Smith. "The festival is going to be here really soon," he added. "What sort of festival? "John Smith said. Now, he could grasp more what Powhatan had to suggest. "The festival to reflect the moment that my citizens will be attending. If I am your Captain." "This is never going to happen! "John Smith screamed. Powhatan wasn't sure of the language the young man spoke. Yet the Chief could see that he was upset with John Smith. "The people have literally no choice!"Powhatan said. "If you don't follow my family, then you have to die! "This is never going to happen! "John Smith screamed. Nobody had ever seen Pocahontas disappear into the longhouse. Powhatan said: "Put a rock on his ear! "John Smith was caught by two big braves and forced his head down on a wall. Powhatan, poised to attack, raised a large rock over him. "Yes!" "The kid screamed. Then, Pocahontas ran forward and leaned over John Smith, raising her own head over him. Powhatan kept the rock in the air high. "And Pocahontas! "He screamed. "Withdraw! "I'm not going to move! "She said, turning her head around sideways. "Please let him is. Let them all be! "The rock was covered up by Powhatan. Then, his wings dropped. "My baby," he said quietly. "You are right. No goodwill comes from harming these men." Powhatan put John Smith at liberty after that. The tribes of Powhatan gave food to the people at the fort again; this time, they roasted meat and pork. In trade, they were offered glass beads and copper by the people at the fort. They shared what they could, and they were both richer for it.

The End.

1.14 A Holy Snake

Years ago, Vishnudutta, a poor Brahmin peasant, stayed in a small village. He had trained hard but couldn't gain much. His wife, Somadutta, has always been demanding more capital. "Be pleased with what you have, my friend," Vishnudutta would claim. One day, after work, Vishnudutta slept in his field. Suddenly, he saw a snake on the surrounding mountain. Seeing Vishnudutta, the snake coiled and stood up with a hood lifted. "It looks so quiet and pleasant. May it be a god," Vishnudutta said. He took from his

house a cup of honey and gave it to the serpent. As Vishnudutta came the next morning to retrieve the cup, he noticed a gold coin in it. "I'm sure it's a holy snake," he said. After that, it was a daily custom for him to give prayers and milk to the snake. And every morning, he got a gold coin in the bowl near the rock, which made Vishnudutta a rich guy. Once, when Vishnudutta was abroad, his son Somadutta had to hold the bowl of milk near the snake. The snake bit Somadutta, and fled. As Vishnudutta came back, his wife said everything to him. "I also warned you of covetousness," Vishnudutta said to his wife. Instead, he fled for the holy snake. He begged forgiveness with clenched hands and gave milk to the sacred snake. Yet this time, the sacred snake did not allow it. "Because of your goodness, I saved your son's life. You will have to compensate for his covetousness. I will no longer help you," said the snake, and vanished.

1.15 A Monkey Judge

Two cats had once been walking through a lane. They immediately noticed a loaf of bread lying under a pine. Everyone pounced on it, and at the same time, captured the sandwich. "They are mine. I noticed it first, "one cat said. While the other said," I pounced on it first, and then it belongs to me. "After battling for a moment, one cat said," Let's split it into two, and take one piece each. "But still, how can we break it? "A monkey seated on the tree branch had seen all that was going with the two animals." That loaf of bread looks fantastic. I should manage that myself, "he said. He came down from the tree cautiously, and then went up to the frightened children. "Hey, my boys! May I help? "The monkey persisted. The cats showed the monkey what the question was and replied, 'Why aren't you the judge between

us?' As the monkey agreed, the cats said, 'Just split this loaf between us.' The smart monkey smilingly cut the bread into two parts, but one slice was a little larger than the other. 'Ah, no! I'm going to take a little bit of the larger slice and make them fair,' the monkey replied slyly. He pulled out the bigger slice of a cookie. Yet, he took a huge slice. "Oh, oh, oh! It has now turned smaller than the other item. I'm just going to have to take a little slice from this portion now, "the sly monkey said. Judge Monkey took another taste. The two cats stood in front of the monkey, watching the loaf of bread they had discovered getting smaller and smaller. Once the monkey had consumed the entire loaf, the monkey replied," I'm sorry. It was very hard to split the loaf. I've got to go now. "If only we had not quarreled with each other, we would have been together, and we would not go to the monkey and get hungry now," the two cats said.

The End

1.16 Adventures of Hercules

Hercules was a hero with strength and bravery. Live in Athens. Hercules had become suspicious of the King. People may transform Hercules into the King. And he decided to get rid of Hercules. He gave Hercules challenging tasks to keep him away from the land so that he might not be a possible danger to him (the King). Hercules once told him to get three golden apples. Several trees were known to grow apples of golden color. They claimed these trees were in a location named Hesperides. Yet no-one understood Hesperides' route. So, the King was worried about Hesperides. Hercules will live apart for a more extended period of time. Hercules started out for the journey. On the voyage, he first encountered three maidens. Hercules asked them about the road to Hesperides. They had asked him to query the sea's old guy. Yet they also cautioned him, "Think closely of the old sea guy. He would otherwise flee. Nobody else knows the path." Hercules noticed the old man. He was asleep on the beach. He appeared odd. He had long hair and a mustache. Hercules moved to him without causing any noise. He then grabbed him very tightly. The old man of the sea opened his eyes. He was startled. He transformed himself into a stag. He struggled to release himself from Hercules' grasp. Ask me the path to Hesperides. "The old man replied," It's a rock, you're going to reach a giant, you're going to take you the path to Hesperides. "Hercules started his quest. He'd interacted with the guy. The giant had been really strong and massive. He was falling asleep on the beach. Hercules had excited him. The giant was indignant. He'd formed a club with Hercules. Hercules has blamed the giant. He raised the giant and go to him set back. Yet the giant quickly backed up. He'd become ten times heavier. Hercules hurled him back and forth again. Yet the giant came up even higher each time. Hercules then raised the giant up high in the air. He wasn't tossing him away. Slowly, the giant lost all of its power. He begged with Hercules now to put him down on earth. Hercules begged Hesperides to inform him of the route. The giant requested that Hercules consult with Atlas. He asked him the path to where Atlas sat. Hercules kept on his ride. In the end, he reached Atlas. "Why do you like the apples golden? "Atlas replied," Hercules said. "My King told me to get these three golden apples from him." "The trip from here to that location is a long way. I will go there, myself. Keep me the moon. I'll have them for you, "Atlas said. Hercules accepted. He kept the sky on his head. Atlas moved out. He was back after a quick time. He set down the three golden apples at the foot of Hercules. Hercules praised Atlas. He begged Atlas to take the sky back from him. "I've kept it for centuries. After another thousand years, I will come here!

"Hercules was shocked by what Atlas asked him, but he didn't show his astonishment. He regained his senses and replied, 'Oh, can you please keep the sky for a little while? I'll make a pad for my hands to help the sky. I'll take the sky back from you.' So Hercules talked very softly. According Atlas. Atlas brought Hercules up into the atmosphere. Hercules obtained the three golden apples straight away. With a mischievous grin on his lips, he told Atlas farewell. The one he flew off to Greece leaving Atlas speechless and confused. Following several days of flying, Hercules entered his birthplace Greece. He'd offered the King the three golden apples. The King was delighted to see Hercules received the golden apples. He was overjoyed. Yet he feigned that he was not pleased. Yet he decided, secretly, to drive Hercules out for another dangerous journey.

The End

1.17 Bravery and its Reward

Courage and its Recognition Once upon a time, there was a good Duke. He was liked by his subjects and valued them.

This Duke had a malevolent uncle. He was called Frederick. Frederick had been rebelling against his uncle. He steered the Duke clear. The Duke was a guy close to goodwill. He fled the Dukedom. He went up to the Arden wood. His supporters went with him too. There he and his family lived a happy life. Frederick was created, Duke. The Duke was to have a baby. She was born in Rosalind. And Frederick had a friend too. She was called Celia. Rosalind and Celia shared a mutual fondness for each other. Celia wished to have Rosalind in the Palace with her. Frederick had allowed Rosalind and his daughter to be in the Palace. To his own Baby, Celia, this was. Sir Rowland De Boys was a relative of the forest-born elder Duke. Sir Rowland died, leaving much of his belongings to his youngest son, Oliver. Oliver has become protective of his younger sibling, named Orlando. Oliver didn't give Orlando any portion of the property or income. He also did not teach Orlando. There was a dominant wrestler in the court of Duke Frederick. Charles was modeled for him. No young man would challenge Charles. Yet Orlando took the task on board. Oliver secretly linked up with Charles. He had told Charles to do Orlando the least. There were several spectators at the wrestling venue. And there was always Duke Frederick. Charles flung tiny challengers one after another in the earlier tournaments. All three of those opponents fractured their ribs. They struggled for survival. It was also where Celia and Rosalind had gone. Duke Frederick told the girls to converse with Orlando, the young guy. Frederick had thought Charles was going to throw down Orlando in the fight. The girls transfer to Orlando. They begged him not to start a war. Orlando politely declined. He said, "I don't need someone to worry about me. I don't even want to die. "The battle ended. Orlando became even heavier than Charles. Orlando raised Charles over his head. And he dropped him away. Charles was exhausted after going down. Frederick and all the others were pleased. Orlando was praised. Orlando said to Frederick," I am the second son of the late Sir Rowland de Boys. "From the point on, Frederick didn't accept Orlando, as they were satisfied. To the opposite, the two girls thanked Orlando. Rosalind became overjoyed. Sit Rowland was a relative of her dad's. She pulled a chain out of her collar and showed it to Orlando. That has been the compensation for his courage.

The End

1.18 Prince and his Carrots

Prince Carrots History most kings and queens once had a presence there. We became princes and princesses. Prince Carrots was one of those Princes. Prince Carrots has become complicated to look at. His head was too wide. He got too big ahead. And his color was orange. He was called Prince Carrots for that purpose. The queen was shocked by the way he felt. His head was too wide. His mouth was far too growing. And she didn't like his head color. "Don't fear," Mercury the Magician said. "The Prince should be really clever. I will bestow a rare favor on him. He should send his intellect to the one he respects the most. "Yet the Prince's smile grew wider each year. The nose grew rising bigger. His

mouth enlarged. And his head became whiter. Yet he was really clever. His wife, the King, placed questions to him. "Have you learned about the Trojan War? "The King demanded. "Dad, of course," said Prince Carrots. "Helen had been abducted by a Trojan named Paris from Greece. Safe in a huge wooden horse is Greek troops. The horse had been taken to Troy's gates. The troops had poured out of the tank, assaulting Troy. They needed Helen to be saved because they loved her. She was really attractive. "His mom, the emperor, even told him questions. "Hence come pearls? "Said the Empress. "By an oyster," said Prince Carrots. "It feels bad when sand comes inside his body. It transforms the sand into a pearl. Only sand will transform stunning. "Prince Carrots might make people laugh too. "The carrots look nice to your skin," he'd say. "Anything except Prince Carrots," should someone say. All had been working desperately not to chuckle. It wasn't cool to make fun of the Prince, who would clearly respond, "Did you ever see a glassed rabbit? "Everyone would chuckle, and the Prince would wave. One day, Prince Carrots waved at a princess from a neighboring country. Prince Carrots saw him look at the queen. He was shocked that he should be stared at by this woman, as she was the most stunning person ever seen. She had a stunning nose. She had good ears. She had a beautiful jaw. Her beauty looked beautiful. There was no way Prince Carrots will turn down. He went to the queen and introduced himself. "I am

Carrots the Duke," he said. "I am Princess Pia," she announced. "I'm pleased to make you here," he added. "It is I who has the pleasure of meeting you," she added. He was astounded. No princess ever got the pleasure of meeting him. "I was told you're a smart man," she said. She didn't wave, though. The queen was frightened. He stood beside her. He said a joke to her, but she wasn't kidding. She had not understood his comment. "Why are you so dishonest? "He was telling her. "I wish I had been clever," she said. "Still, you're really cute," he added. "Yes," she announced. "I've read it a thousand times," Princess Pia said a tale to Prince Carrots. She'd learned the story 1,000 times. She only heard things after she referred to them a thousand times. "My mum has a relative of a wizard," said the girl. "She told him when I was little, that she was worried about me. I was cute, but I wasn't really clever." "You're pretty good, "said the boy. "Though not really intellectual," the princess said. "My mum needed him to make me wiser. He told her there was no chance he could. He was not enough to give me someone I was not. He asked her that I'd love for my appearance." "What happens afterward? "The Prince was concerned. "Oh, always concerned about my mum," she said. "The magician promised her he'd send me a treat. He said I should only send someone my talent. I should give it to the person I valued the most. "Again, the Prince nodded. He had received a similar present from Mercury. Prince Carrots and Princess

Pia were both pretty much alike. The Prince and the princess had been enjoying the day together. Prince Carrots has learned the tale several times about Mercury the Witch. The princess was unable to recall she had already asked him about it. Yet they didn't miss Prince Carrots. The princess had noticed out the boy was a pleasant listener. Yet he has been difficult to look at. He didn't appear to care as she looked away. He grinned brightly. She really enjoyed it. The Prince was fond of staring at the bride. He liked the way that he thought about her too. She wasn't answering many questions. She didn't want to be asking him stories. When he was with her, he was not feeling bad. The princess enjoyed the feeling she got regarding the Prince. And the Prince feels just the same way. "You are very affectionate to me," said the Prince. "You too are very close to me," said the queen. Prince Carrots lost out on Princess Pia when they were split. He could not breathe until he met her. Princess Pia had not been able to wait to see the boy. She was still alert to be with him. "Even though her hair gets messy, she is stunning," the Prince figured. "He's smart to say stuff, and I recall," figured the queen. "They're going to date me? "One day, the Prince inquired. He just couldn't control himself. Princess Pia was always too good. "Yes."... Yes! "Said the queen. She just couldn't support herself. Prince Carrots was always too smart. When they heard the report, everyone was stunned. No one except Mercury the Magician may believe it. He realized that, when we are in love, we are exactly what we want to be. We are genuinely valued for what we are.

1.19 A Good Baby

The child was in a position to go to bed. Mum and dad comfortably put him in his bed. They made sure they put the night-light on and lit the house with its warm glow. Mom and dad stayed in the doorway and gave Baby's kisses before tiptoeing down the corridor. "Good dreams, Baby! "Daddy said. But there was just one minor question. Missing his teddy bear, Baby did not go to sleep - and Teddy did not be found anywhere! The child asked what they were going to do. His first reaction that he would start weeping. When he began to weep, mom and dad will certainly rush to the nursery and see what the problem was. Yet Baby did not want to offend mum and dad. He wasn't exactly whether to convince everyone he'd lose his Teddy too. And Baby did not want to scream. He also will have to locate Teddy. Babysat up in his crib, hanging on tightly to the bars for support. Babysat up very well in his crib, but he was always too small to get out. Baby has been searching for the nursery to see how he might spy on his Teddy. Elsewhere, keen-eared Puppy, out in the corridor, heard Baby stirring in his crib. The puppy came for a tour bounding for the nursery. Puppy pressed his snout against the door, and, with a creek, it flew open. Puppy flew into the room and happily wagged his ears. The baby was delighted to see his Puppy mate. Baby wished

Puppy could help him look for Teddy because Puppy could walk easily around the nursery while Baby was reluctant to leave his crib. Baby wanted to say Puppy he'd gone to locate his Teddy. Sadly, Baby has always not been very successful at chatting. The puppy was not very successful at knowing things, either. And Puppy became really enthusiastic when Baby raised his arms and made tiny noises. He thought Baby preferred just to dance! Soon, here and there, Puppy was jumping, running over toys, and causing such a commotion. Sshhh, Baby! Puppy looked on the floor so cute jumping about, and the Baby began giggling a little. The baby then began chuckling. The baby then began laughing a fat big belly laugh! The baby was laughing so intensely and sincere that he had to pause for a moment. While chuckling, Baby ended up in his crib on the warm quilt. As Baby was sleeping and worrying about that dumb Dog, he found his crèche looked oddly lumpy and bumpy. The baby was really interested in that. He moved onto the quilt. It looked like there might be something cuddly and sweet beneath! The child gently pulled the quilt off. Do you remember what he saw? One small brown ear. Then, a small brown ear.

Suddenly there was a fuzzy brown hair, two nice little heads, and a large gentle nose... it was Teddy! He and Baby had been in the crib all along! So happy it was a boy. The baby snuggled next to his teddy bear and felt very warm and safe. Suddenly Baby was getting ready to fall asleep. He closed his little head and slept soundly in no time. Good night, Baby.

1.20 Gretal and Hansel Story

Once a boy called Hansel and his sister Gretel had stayed in a small cottage on the outskirts of a thick forest with their mother. Their dad was a woodcutter. Though there was often plenty of firewood in the family to keep their home warm and comfortable, there was also not enough food. Indeed, several times for their dinner, Hansel and Gretel had little but a slice of bread. Night after night, well after Hansel and Gretel had gone to bed, and their parents would sit down at the table, contemplating the future of the household. And when they talked, they also could hear Hansel and Gretel talking. "What would become of us? "Daddy inquired. "We won't even have enough resources for flour enough," Mother said. "We'll manage." "We're still seeking something to survive." "We're all going to starve to death when I travel to the forest to find jobs," Father sighed. "Don't do anything like this," Mother wept. "With nobody selling my wood to," continued Dad, "we have little income. We can't buy food without resources. Which other choice do we have? I can't wait to see my kids find jobs! "Mom was only gasping at the idea. "If you understand," said Dad, squeezing his head, "I'll go through the forest to find jobs, and we'll have something to feed." "Enough for one night," said Mother peacefully. "They're a woodcutter. A trustworthy woodcutter who works hard.

We're trying to find a way to handle it. Now let us get some time." "Hansel, get you heard? "Gretel talked in the dark to her uncle. "So I learned," Hansel said. "I don't want to let Father go," she added. "What is it we should do? "I'm going to leave," said Hansel. "How are you going to go? "Asked by Gretel. "To find work, I'll ride through the wood," Hansel said softly. "Then, I will come with you," Gretel said. "Don't be dumb," joked Hansel. "Forests are a dangerous place. "If the forest is too risky," Gretel said, "you will need my assistance." "Gretel, you're incredibly stubborn. Well then, "said Hansel getting out of his bunk. "We'll depart tomorrow." Hansel and Gretel hurried out of bed before dawn and then threw on their clothing until their parents were up. Gretel grabbed some bread from the kitchen and put it in her pockets. "And on our trip, we're not going to die," she said. "I think it's not such a terrible thing for you to come along," Hansel said as he guided his sister out the door and through the dark wood. "Well done, father and mum," whispered Gretel. The kids moved along quietly. We marched across the thick brush and tall trees the entire day. They walked until their feet hurt." I did not know that the forest was so big, "Gretel said." Not either, "Hansel said. "For long, it'll be dusk. Are you afraid? "Just scared? "Gretel said with a smile. "I? Why should I think about? "I just thought," stammered Hansel, "maybe you decided to go back home. If you were worried, it's not too late for us to turn around." Maybe you're a little nervous, buddy, "Gretel said." Don't be

dumb. I'm tired, but I'm not scared, "Hansel said." It's a good thing you don't want to turn around, "Gretel said, gazing about her." I'm curious which direction is home anyway." "Don't think about it, "Hansel said confidently laughing. "We are not defeated. This saddens me. I left behind us a trail of bread crumbs, just in case we have to turn back." You're really funny, Hansel, "Gretel laughed." You laugh after I lost my precious bread to save us?" "Hansel, we should split my cookies," said Gretel laughing again. "What's so funny? "I'm afraid if I say you," Gretel said sadly, "you're going to be terrified. It's better if I don't answer you." I won't move a step forward before you answer me, "ordered Hansel. Gretel went on." Wait! "Hansel flew by his sister's side. "Poor girl! Didn't you promise me you'd split your food? I am tired! "Dear Dad, I'm afraid you've traded for nothing of your precious food," Gretel said as she walked." What? "Asked Hansel." Look! "And Gretel said, looking at him. "That's why I'm laughing." Three blackbirds flew by them, slowly collecting every bit of bread crumb that Hansel left off. Hansel's path had vanished for them. "Hansel, here take some," Gretel said, holding out a slice of bread for her dad. "I'm no longer hungry," Hansel replied, and moved away. They will probably come across someone, or somewhere they could rest and eat something sweet. Now they looked like they were wandering in circles. Night dropped on the trees. Strange sounds also come from behind the bushes. Hansel and Gretel remained huddled and whispered against the cold." Have you noticed that? "Hansel tried to search for Gretel's hand." Tonight I learned so many things," muttered Gretel. "We will sleep and seek. We're going to get up in the morning and travel the entire day before we make our way through." But I'm really hungry now, "Hansel said." Tell me, Hansel," Gretel said, digging through her pockets again, "what job are you planning to do on the other end of the forest? "I want to be a peasant," muttered Hansel. "I'm trying to produce so much food that we're never trying to hunger again. Now, Gretel, what kind of job are you planning to do? "Gretel was worrying about it for a moment. Before she could speak, Hansel and Gretel both fell asleep. Gretel dreamt of being sat by their cozy fire and dining with her children. They were consuming onions, lettuce, carrots, and beans, all planted by the farmer Hansel. We kept out throughout the morning. We first have sung songs that their parents taught them to help pass the time. Both quickly became exhausted and hungry again and moved slowly along." Gretel, look! "Hansel screamed. A Farmhouse! "Kids couldn't believe their heads. A small cottage stood there in a small clearing. "Maybe whoever lives in that cottage will give us some food," Hansel said. "Let's hope," Gretel said, running towards the small building. The walls have been built from gingerbread! Colorful candies tiled the roof and the windowpanes built of pure sugar." It is the most amazing building I've ever seen! "Gretel said." It's the best house I've ever seen! "Wait," Gretel screamed, "we will see if someone is home and check before we eat." Hansel knocked at the cookie door. But nobody answered." Knock again," Gretel. Both knocked and yelled out." Tip-tap, tap-tap, who's rapping at my door?" "Said an angry man." The sky, the sky, there's nothing but the storm," the man frightened the men. The door to the building right then opened, and a very elderly lady with a walking stick walked out. The old woman sweetly replied, "Do not stress. Come in." We flew through the forest without consuming something," said Gretel. "We're desperately hungry." Kids, you've come to the right spot," joked the old lady. "Help yourself. Load your bellies with sugar, then come in then take a rest." The old woman cooked a meal of pancakes with rich syrup for Hansel and Gretel. She spilled large amounts of milk on them. As they fed, they told her about their woodland trip. They assured her they had ambitions to pursue jobs. The old woman grinned. "You are such nice people. And the forest is such a risky sport! Move on now; I built beds for you. Rest for your trip." She gave them two little beds that were lightly wrapped. "I wonder what job I'm going to do at the other end of the park," Gretel said. "I'm going to learn how to create lovely houses made of sweets, desserts and big candies." You may need my assistance," Hansel said, nodding off to sleep. Before the kids woke, the old woman caught Hansel and shut him up in a tiny cage. Then she switched to the now sleeping Gretel. "Wake up; you're lazy, go get some water to prepare something decent for your dad. I'm going to feed him when he's big enough," the woman said. "It has to be a cigar! "She said. "She's a sorcerer! "Hansel screamed from inside the cage." That's true," exclaimed the sorceress. "I'm a wizard, and you're my supper." The witch made sure Hansel had enough to feed over the next few weeks. She decided to see him get very, very big. She stood at his cage every morning and said, "Put your finger out, so that I can see how plump you are! "But Hansel was clever and courageous. He realized witches are not seen very well. He held out a small little chicken bone instead of his finger, which Gretel had managed to subtly slip through him." Hmmm," the witch said as she felt the chicken bone. "What a cute little thing you are! You ought to stop getting something! "Then at Gretel, she begged to bring some food to Hansel. In the meantime, Gretel was provided only bread crusts to consume. While the old witch rested in her cozy bed at night, and Gretel lay down in the kitchen corner, the two kids would sing quietly the songs they had learned from their mother. After four weeks had elapsed and Hansel always appeared to be very lean, the old witch lost all her composure. She could no longer sit. Gretel," she shouted. "Rapid! Use enough hot water. If Hansel is heavy or lean, I'll roast him and feed him this morning! "Yes! No!" "Gretel shouted." You stubborn girl, do as I'm doing and do it now," ordered the old witch, banging her cane on the concrete floor. Gretel didn't move." Fine," said the witch, "if that's how you like it, I'll eat you for dessert! "Gretel was now not going. The witch was still really mad. "I've already heated the oven first, and then kneaded the flour." She nudged Gretel up to the oven. "Creep in, and see if the bread is hot enough." Gretel realized he didn't believe the old woman. "Sorry," Gretel eventually replied, "I don't know how to check." You stubborn goose," the witch screamed, "Do what I say." I won't," Gretel replied bravely." Then get out of my path, and I'm going to do everything myself. True.